The Compassion of Captain Cook

John Webber, *Portrait of a New Zealander*, 1777
pen and ink with watercolour
(Dixon Library, State Library of New South Wales, Sydney, Pe 214)

Kahoura sat in the long cabin and posed for this portrait, a sign of peaceful reconciliation, after the meeting with Cook on February 24.

The Compassion of Captain Cook

Christopher Heathcote

Connor Court Publishing Pty Ltd

Published in 2023 by Connor Court Publishing Pty Ltd.

Copyright © Christopher Heathcote, 2023.

All rights reserved.

Not to be reproduced without the permission of the Copyright holders.

Connor Court Publishing Pty Ltd.
PO Box 7257
Redland Bay QLD 4165
sales@connorcourt.com
www.connorcourt.com

ISBN: 9781922815309

Cover Design by Maria Giordano.

COVER IMAGE: Disregarding his own safety, Cook stands among hostile natives and signals his men to cease fire. (Detail from John Webber, The Death of Captain Cook, engraving, 1784 edition. Courtesy State Library of New South Wales, DL Pf 61)

Printed in Australia.

Contents

About the author	vii
Preface	ix
1. The Compassion of Captain Cook	1
2. Paper Trails	47
3. Pictorial Records	79
Index	103

A debonair Lt Phillips responds to native attack on the tropical beach. Modelled by Webber and Bartolozzi upon classical sculpture familiar to cultured viewers, the officer's reclining pose conveys an Apollo-like ease merged with Herculean power. (Detail from *The Death of Captain Cook*, 1782. see pp.94ff)

About the Author

Christopher Heathcote (PhD) is an author of several books, art critic, and authority on Australian art. In a chequered career he has been art critic for *The Age*, associate editor of *Art Monthly Australia*, an academic at La Trobe and Melbourne Universities then the Victorian College of the Arts, a curator of exhibitions at regional galleries and Canberra's National Gallery, as well as head of the Gordon Institute's art school.

Dr Heathcote is co-author with professors Bernard Smith and Terry Smith of *Australian Painting 1788-2000*, acclaimed as the 'classic' account of Australian art. He has written two definitive histories, *A Quiet Revolution: The Rise of Australian Art 1946-1968*, and *Inside the Art Market: Australia's Galleries 1956-1976*. And several pioneering monographs, including *Russell Drysdale: Defining the Modern Australian Landscape*, *Discovering Dobell* and *The Art of Roger Kemp*. He is a contributor to the *Australian Dictionary of Biography*.

Also by Christopher Heathcote

A Quiet Revolution: The Rise of Australian Art 1946-1968
The Art of Roger Kemp
Defining the Modern Australian Landscape: Russell Drysdale
Discovering Dobell
Inside the Art Market: Australia's Galleries, A History
The Exhibition Handbook
A Century of Roses: The Rose Society of Victoria

With Bernard Smith & Terry Smith
Australian Painting 1788-2000

With Patrick McCaughey & Sarah Thomas
Encounters with Modern Australian Art

With Bruce Adams
Yvonne Audette: Paintings & Drawings

With Jenny Zimmer & Charles Nodrum
George Johnson: Worldview

Preface

This short book is ostensibly about James Cook's relations with Pacific natives in light of the two massacres that were inflicted upon his expeditions.

It was prompted by my curiosity about two works of art by John Webber, the artist travelling on the last voyage.

James Cook is now the subject of highly politicised arguments. Severe claims are circulating about his motives in exploring the Pacific, and how he conducted himself there. People who style themselves as progressively-minded now ignore altogether the scientific importance of those expeditions, and even call for the removal of public memorials to the navigator-scientist.

The visual works considered here—*Portrait of a New Zealander*, and *The Death of Captain Cook*—bear directly on what is currently being said against Cook. Writers of history can devote scant attention to pictures, treating them as ornaments to adorn a book. But these two works have evidential value. They were made by the professional illustrator who accompanied the third Pacific voyage to record for perpetuity what took place. I trust the reader finds what I write about them germane to the debate underway.

Art historians well know how these studies evolve. One's interest is stimulated by a drawing or picture, so you do some checks to find out more. Ready information is lean. So, next thing, you are digging through old records. Depending on the art concerned, you may begin grappling with weighty issues, looking at historical events via an unexpected viewpoint: 'Art matters a great deal,' the painter Francis Bacon used to say, 'because all the greatest aspirations of the human race have been left to us in art.'

I would add this study is a by-product of my city's Covid lockdowns of 2020-21. The management of that pandemic was inconvenient for us all, at moments quite frightening; but I was able to use the months of restrictions on movement to research and write this work.

Even though my labours mostly took place in enforced isolation I am indebted to certain individuals and organisations for assisting me in various ways. So I thank the staff at the National Library of Australia, the State Library of New South Wales, the State Library of Victoria, and (via email) the British Museum. The artist Andrew Christofides and printmaker Caterina Poljski helped with specialised information at some points. Keith Windschuttle published an early shorter version of the study in *Quadrant* magazine. I am especially grateful to Anthony Cappello of Connor Court who has seen the book progress into print.

When quoting Cook himself in this study I have used J.C. Beaglehole (editor) *The Journals of Captain James Cook on his Voyages of Discovery*, published for the Hakluyt Society by the University Press at Cambridge. When referring to related works of art I have used the catalogue raissone published by Rüdiger Joppien and Bernard Smith as *The Art of Captain Cook's Voyages* by Oxford University Press. As well D.W. Orchiston & L.C. Horrocks's article 'Contact and Conflict: The Rowe Massacre,' in the journal *Historical Studies* (17: 1975, pp.519-38), is taken as the authorative account of what transpired in that tragic incident.

CH. Keilor Plains, 2022

The Compassion of Captain Cook

> … that best portion of a good man's life;
> His little, nameless, unremembered acts
> Of kindness and of love.
>
> Wordsworth, *Tintern Abbey*

As sailors shoot at agitated natives, Lt Williamson runs the launch close in to the beach and rescues wounded marines.
(Detail from *The Death of Captain Cook*, 1782. see pp.94ff)

James Cook, the finest maritime explorer in recorded history, was among the victims of a violent attack by indigenous peoples. His murder and those of four marines protecting him, as well as the brutal deaths of another ten crewmen on his previous expedition, may be omitted from postmodern lists of historic massacres in the Pacific region. Nevertheless, what transpired on both occasions were massacres.

The first killings occurred in New Zealand during the expedition of 1772-75. Recently promoted to Commander, James Cook was leading two vessels: his own ship *HMS Resolution,* and *HMS Adventure* captained by Commander Tobias Furneaux. Cook used them in tandem to explore and map the southern Indian Ocean and the South Pacific, searching for land at high latitudes while aspiring to approach the South Pole.

By late October 1773 the ships had completed a first segment of their mission and looped back to New Zealand's Queen Charlotte Sound for food, water and periodic maintenance. Cook quickly arrived at this staging point and waited for Furneaux who was delayed by a storm. The *Adventure* hadn't appeared after three weeks, so, unwilling to linger, the *Resolution* headed off on November 23 to take advantage of summer weather. The *Adventure* arrived a week later and made rushed repairs at the anchorage. On its last day at this stopover, Furneaux sent a party headed by Midshipman James Rowe to forage for scurvy-grass, wild celery and edible greens. They had not returned by sundown. This was in Wharehunga Bay on December 17.[1]

The next morning Furneaux sent a second group, led by Lieutenant James Burney and including ten marines, to find those who had disappeared. After an extensive search they were horrified to find on a beach body parts of some missing crewmen, along with human flesh already cooked.

In the next cove they noticed a Maori gathering. Led by

---

[1] For a full description see D.W. Orchiston & L.C. Horrocks, 'Contact and Conflict: The Rowe Massacre,' *Historical Studies,* 17 (1975), pp. 519-38.

the chief Kahura, the Maoris were conducting a *whangai hau* ceremony where warriors eat parts of an enemy to absorb his spirit. After driving off the Maoris with gunfire, Burney found more butchered remains. None of the crewmen's bodies were intact, his group recovering two hands (one belonging to Rowe), the head of the captain's Negro servant, assorted bones, plus torn trousers, a frock coat, and six odd shoes. The deceased numbered two midshipmen (James Rowe and Thomas Woodhouse), the quartermaster (Francis Murphy), Furneaux's servant (James Sevilley), and six sailors (Michael Bell, John Cavenaugh, William Facey, Thomas Hill, Edward Jones, Thomas Milton).[2]

The second massacre occurred on the subsequent scientific expedition of 1776-79. Now raised to the rank of Post-Captain, James Cook again was leading two vessels: his own ship *HMS Resolution,* and *HMS Discovery* captained by Commander Charles Clerke who had served on both his previous expeditions. Cook used the ships to explore the north-eastern Pacific, scouring the Canadian coast for a 'North-West' sea passage from the Atlantic Ocean.

Over the warmer Arctic months of 1778 the ships explored and mapped parts of the west coast of Canada and Alaska, and the Bering Sea. Cook planned to rest his crews in the tropics for the northern winter, before returning to complete mapping the region from spring onward. So the ships made for the Hawaiian Islands which the expedition had happened upon a year earlier. The two and a half month visit was initially pleasant, but by February 1779 the mariners had overstayed their welcome. Tensions were strained, with pilfering and harassment by natives getting out of hand: 'we have observ'd in the Natives a stronger propensity to theft,' Clerke recorded. 'Every day produc'd more numerous and

---

[2] In his journal Lieutenant James Burney records Sevilley as Swilley. Suzanne Rickard, *Sailing with Cook: Inside the Private Journal of James Burney RN*, National Library of Australia, Canberra, 2015, p. 117.

more audacious depridations.'[3] For this reason February 12 saw all Hawaiians ordered off both ships, although that afternoon one climbed onto the *Resolution* where, startling the crew on deck, he grabbed what he could then dived into the sea and got away. Using the word *insolent*, Cook was exasperated.[4]

Then, overnight, the cutter was stolen. It had been well secured to the *Resolution*, but a four inch rope was cut through. The theft was critical. With an attachable mast, which meant it could be sailed, the cutter was effectively a swift utility runabout. Cook had been using this six-oared large rowboat for navigating shoals, ice floes and precision mapping, as well as rowing ahead with the launch and towing a ship if becalmed in hazardous waters. Its loss meant there were now only four boats (a pinnace, a launch, a small cutter and the light Jolly boat or yawl), all slower and less effective when pressing work was at hand.

Cook acted instantly after the theft was discovered. Early in the morning he led a shore party of ten marines to see Kalaniʻopuʻu, the island's aged leader. When wakened in his hut the chief proved unaware of the theft. So Cook decided to take him hostage until the cutter was returned. The party led Kalaniʻopuʻu toward the beach. Halfway there agitated natives began surrounding them. Cook said to Lieutenant Phillips of the marines 'We can never think of compelling him to go onboard without killing a number of those People,' and released the chief.[5] This was in Kealakekua Bay, at 8.00am on February 14.

The outnumbered Europeans were attacked at the shoreline. A native made to jab at Cook with an iron spike, so, giving the order to fire, the navigator fired his own musket loaded with small

---

[3] J.C. Beaglehole (editor), *The Journals of Captain James Cook on His Voyages of Discovery, Vol.3: The Voyage of the* Resolution *and* Discovery *1776-1780*, Cambridge, at the University Press, for the Hakluyt Society, 1967, pt. 1, p. 531.

[4] The thief made away with a chisel, the armorer's tongs, and the lid of a storage cask for the ship's salt supply. Beaglehole, *Journals of Cook*, vol. 3, pt. 1, pp. 529, 531, and pt. 2, pp. 1359-60.

[5] Beaglehole, *Journals of Cook*, vol. 3, pt. 1, p. 535.

shot. The pellets merely stuck in the native's clothing wrap. Next thing Cook called out 'Take to the boats,' although the chance had passed: according to Phillips 'the business was now a most miserable scene of confusion—the Shouts and the Yells of the Indians far exceeded all the noise I ever came in the way of.'[6] As the marines fought, Phillips saw Cook clubbed from behind then turn and with his musket's second barrel shoot this attacker dead at the waters edge. This was his moment to flee, but Cook could not swim. He had never learned how. Other natives beat him, stabbed his neck then shoved him under the waves. They kept on stabbing until he stopped moving. Unable to reload their muskets, others in the party were clubbed and knifed, before swimming to the launch which Lieutenant Williamson brought close in. All the while rowboats off the beach attempted covering fire, watched by crew on the two ships at anchor in the bay. The natives had killed four marines in the affray (Privates John Allen, Thomas Fatchett, Theophilus Hinks, and Corporal James Thomas).

How did the respective naval commanders respond to this native violence? Tobias Furneaux delayed taking action straight after the 1773 massacre in New Zealand. For safety's sake, no further party was sent ashore from his ship, while an increased watch was posted overnight to keep an eye out for canoes.

In this Furneaux was observing Admiralty practice. Anchored close offshore, the *Adventure* was vulnerable; and a captain's duty was to protect his vessel and crew. Not that the officers and Jack tars were emboldened to take reprisals. The cannibalism panicked them. Their anxieties were amplified by wet weather which made firearms unreliable. When volleys were attempted after the butchered bodies were discovered, four marines in Lieutenant Burney's party had muskets misfire. This enabled the Maoris to flee, so all the shore party could do is disable three canoes drawn up on the beach to prevent pursuit.

---

[6] Beaglehole, *Journals of Cook*, vol. 3, pt. 1, pp. 535-6.

The next morning Furneaux had resolved not only to avoid further contact with Maoris, but to abandon the expedition altogether. Mind you, his departure fits with a pattern of overcaution on the expedition, Furneaux repeatedly testing Cook's patience by holding back in bad weather and iceberg-ridden waters. Upon leaving Kealakekua Bay, the *Adventure* did not aim to rejoin the *Resolution* at either of Cook's planned stops on Easter Island or Tahiti. Instead, Furneaux sailed for the Atlantic, and then onward to Britain.

Charles Clerke assumed command of the expedition after the 1778 massacre in Hawaii, taking measures to protect both ships and their crews. He called the rowboats to return. An observatory had been set up along the beach, and the ships' carpenters had a workshop there, too. Clerke had Lieutenant King, Cook's subordinate on the *Resolution*, lead a group to retrieve the meteorological and astronomical equipment, carpenter's tools and a replacement foremast being readied for the *Resolution*. A squad of marines repelled several natives on the beach who attacked as this evacuation was underway.

By 11.30am all were back aboard, and Clerke had the two vessels move further along the shore. There was now among the crew talk of vengeance. Lieutenant Bligh had observed via telescope natives cutting up the European corpses, so cannibalism was feared. The *Discovery* several times fired a cannon at the village and adjacent coconut grove. 'I had some notion of taking a stout party onshore, make what distruction among them I could, then burn the Town, Canoes & c,' Clerke admitted in his journal, but 'I thought it would be improper.'[7] The pressure on Clerke, who was visibly dying of tuberculosis, was great. Yet he forbade reprisals, reiterating the expedition's rule of minimal response to violence. He knew Cook would not have allowed pay-back. The deceased captain made this abundantly clear months earlier when they

---
[7] Ibid., p. 540.

revisited the locality where Maoris massacred Furneaux's sailors. Clerke added, as practical justification, it would be 'probably injurious to the expedition to risk further loss of the People.'[8]

The journals of the ships' officers reveal discipline problems that afternoon and next morning. Commander Clerke was so ill he rested in his cabin. Without permission, some tars went ashore where they burned huts and shot at natives, killing two men then mutilating their corpses. 'In every instance it was not in the power of the Officers to restrain them,' wrote the appalled Lieutenant King.[9] There was also taunting by certain Hawaiians. Midshipman Harvey on the *Resolution* recorded how on the beach 'the lower class was insulting, who strutted about with our peoples Jacketts & Trouzers on, other flourishing Cutlashes, Hangers & Bayonets, defieing us to come ashore… some of them was seen to turn up their naked breach' [that is expose their backsides to the ships] but 'we were not to fire at them.'[10]

Then chiefs appeared bearing white flags and gifts of food, making gestures to meet. Lieutenants King and Burney rowed over in a boat, and spoke with them from the water. (This was the same James Burney who discovered the New Zealand massacre four years earlier.) 'The Chiefs during the parley behav'd very well,' Harvey added, 'not the least appearance of treachery among them.'[11] There was sincere talk of peace and the officers explained they needed to recover the captain's body. Clerke himself was now sure native violence was unintended, writing he

> must leave it to superior Judgments to settle the secret springs and original causes of action, with once more observing that the unhappy catastrophe which befell us I do not think appears by no means the effect of premeditated intention, but of an unfortunate string of circumstances …[12]

---

[8] Beaglehole, *Journals of Cook*, vol. 3, pt. 1, p. 540.
[9] Ibid., p. 562.
[10] Ibid., p. 541, footnote.
[11] Ibid.
[12] Ibid., pp. 593-4.

The next day an envoy from Kalaniʻopuʻu arrived under a flag of truce. He was allowed on ship. Expressing profound shame for the attack, the Hawaiian was aghast at being suspected of cannibalism. He explained how out of reverence for Cook—who natives mistook for either a chief or a god—funeral rites were already underway. The body had been ceremonially divided, with parts distributed among tribal leaders according to ritual. So Clerke used this envoy to send a message, chief-to-chief, promising no further violence while demanding the captain's remains.[13]

All had not calmed down. There were still provocative gestures by fragmented native groups, as Lieutenant Burney noted:

> About 2 in the afternoon a Small Canoe came from the town of Kavarooa and Stopped near the Resolution. after looking at her some minutes, an Indian in the middle of the canoe stood up and put Captain Cooks hat on, making many flourishes and antick gestures expressive of defiance and derision. he was fired at and a boat manned to chase him, on which he made towards the Shore where he was received with great Shoutings by a crowd of Indians. 3 Great Guns were fired which dispersed them.[14]

Over three days the Hawaiians returned most of Cook's bones, some flesh, along with items of his clothing and personal equipment. In accordance with the natives' funeral rites, his missing bones had already been left in most sacred places. Clerke then felt able to conduct a burial at sea. Flags flew at half mast, bells were tolled, a ten gun salute fired, and the catafalque slid into the sea. The *Resolution*'s new foremast was stepped the next morning, then the two vessels set sail. The remains of the deceased marines were not recovered.

James Cook's response to the deaths of Furneaux's sailors in New Zealand had been necessarily delayed. The *Resolution* made

---

[13] The envoy reported to Clerke that 25 natives had died in the violence three days before.

[14] James Burney, *Journey on HMS Discovery 10 Feb. 1776 – 24 Aug. 1779*, Safe 1/64; Safe 1/79, Mitchell Library, State Library of NSW, vol. 4, p. 2.

another stopover at Queen Charlotte Sound in late October 1774, but Maoris were evasive when sailors asked after the *Adventure*. Some heard rumours that a ship had been wrecked in the Sound, and survivors killed by natives. Suspicions were raised after one Maori 'receiv'd a box on the ear' from his friends for referring to a vessel in conversation with Cook's crew: 'whenever I questioned the natives about it they always dinied all knowledge of it,' he noted in his journal. 'These stories made me vy uneasy about the Adventure and I desired Mr Wales and those on Shore to let me know if any of the Natives should mention it again...'[15]

Cook learned more the following March when, on his return voyage to Britain, the *Resolution* was overtaken in the Indian Ocean by a Dutch merchant ship out of Bengal. Its captain, Cornelis Bosch, said a tale was circulating that one of the *Adventure*'s boats had been dashed to pieces in New Zealand, then natives had killed and eaten all survivors.[16] Besides rocketing around seaports, the disturbing news had sparked a sensation in Britain. This was over 18 months since Cook's last sight of the *Adventure*: 'the story which we heard in Queen Charlotte's Sound was no longer to be doubted,' he noted.[17] Days later the *Resolution* reached Cape Town. An explanatory letter left by Commander Furneaux was awaiting Cook there.

At the same stopover the navigator heard details of an altercation on a French expedition to the Pacific, which stopped at New Zealand's Bay of Islands in mid 1772. Natives there had massacred and eaten the navigator Marc-Joseph Marion du Fresne and twenty-six sailors. (On first hearing of this cannibalism Jean-Jacques Rousseau, author of the 'Noble Savage' theory, was shaken: 'Is it possible,' he blurted out, 'that the good Children of Nature

---

[15] J.C. Beaglehole (editor), *The Journals of Captain James Cook on His Voyages of Discovery, Vol. 2: The Voyage of the* Resolution *and* Adventure *1772-1775*, Cambridge, at the University Press, for the Hakluyt Society, 1969, pp. 572-3.
[16] Beaglehole, *Journals of Cook,* vol. 2, p. 652.
[17] Ibid.

can really be so wicked?'[18]) Brutal reprisals followed, the French killing 250 Maoris and incinerating a village.

Cook was also troubled in Cape Town to read parts of a book *An Account of the Voyages undertaken... for making Discoveries in the Southern Hemisphere* (1773). Commissioned by the Admiralty from the fashionable *litterateur* John Hawkesworth, this work very freely used Cook's and Banks's *Endeavour* journals to recycle European dreams of fantastic and exotic peoples. Patagonian natives were giants, Dr Hawkesworth opined, while Tahiti was a cross between classical idyll and land of free love. The inaccuracies on natives worried Cook greatly.

Reaching safe harbour at The Downs, Kent, in July 1775, Cook went up to London and proceeded to curb talk of his most recent expedition encountering barbaric cannibals. He read the *Adventure*'s journal, meeting with some of the crew, and received a fuller account of what did happen at Queen Charlotte Sound. The navigator's precise thoughts on these matters at this time we do not know.

And Cook now learned Hawkesworth's book—parts of which had been serialised in the *Gentleman's Magazine*—was not as well regarded as he feared. Various readers declared it irreligious, in bad taste, lewd, pompous and boring. Joseph Banks was in two minds: if the book heroised him, it twisted his careful observations. This probably was to be expected as Hawkesworth had done similar when editing Swift's letters, rewriting years of correspondence. James Boswell, who later met Cook at a dinner party, found the navigator annoyed by how the author took to trite generalising about Pacific natives on scant evidence: 'He has used your narrative as a London tavern keeper does wine,' Boswell sympathised. 'He has brewed it.'[19]

---

[18] Bernard Smith, *European Vision and the South Pacific* (1960), Oxford University Press, Oxford, 1989, p. 123.
[19] This was after Cook's second Pacific voyage, at a dinner given by Sir John Pringle on 2 April 1776. Boswell related the conversation to Samuel Johnson the following day, outlining the liberties Hawkesworth had taken with Cook's journal. James Boswell, *Life of Johnson* (1791), Oxford World's Classics, Oxford, 1998, pp. 722-3.

A year and a half later, in early 1777, James Cook was back at Queen Charlotte Sound, site of the *Adventure* tragedy. He was now leading a third Pacific expedition, with his dependable protégé Charles Clerke managing the consort vessel. Maoris appeared when the *Resolution* and *Discovery* anchored together.[20] Cook's journal for February 11 runs:

> We had not been long at anchor before several Canoes filled with natives came alongside the Ships, but very few of them would venture on board; which appeared the more extraordinary as I was well known to them all. There was one man amongst them that I had treated with remarkable kindness during my whole stay when I was last here, yet now neither professions of friendship nor presents would induce him to come into the ship. It appeared to me that they were apprehensive we were come to revenge the death of Captain Furneaux's people.[21]

Using a Tahitian aboard, Omai, as translator, Cook tried to re-establish amicable relations:

> I did all in my power to assure them of the continuance of my friendship, and that I should not disturb them on that account. I do not know whether this had any weight with them; but certain it is that they soon laid aside allmanner of restraint and distrust.[22]

On February 13 the expedition pitched tents and established a shore camp. Fresh water and greens were obtained, spruce beer was brewed, a group harvested vegetables sown on the previous visit, observatories were set up and ships' maintenance began. Cook ordered that all working ashore be armed, with a guard of ten marines constantly protecting the camp, while Lieutenant King and three petty officers supervised shore activities. The journal continues:

> A boat was never sent to any considerable distance from the Ships without being armed, and under the direction of such officers as

---

[20] Beaglehole, *Journals of Cook*, vol. 3, pt. 1, p. 59.
[21] Ibid.
[22] Ibid.

I could depend upon and who were well acquainted with the Natives. Some of these precautions I had never taken before in this place; nor were they, I firmly beleive, more necessary now, but after the sacrifice which the Natives made of the boats crew belonging to the Adventure in this place, and the French in the Bay of Islands it was totally impossible, totally, to divest ourselves of apprehinsions of the same nature. If the Natives had any suspicion of our revenging these acts of Barbarity they very soon laid it aside, for during the course of this day a great many Families came from different parts and took up their residence by us, so that there was not a place in the Cove where a Hut could be built that was not occupied by some or another: the place where we had fixed our little incampment they left us in quiet possession of; but they came and took away the remains of some old huts that were there.[23]

Placed under strict orders never to quarrel, let alone trade blows with any native, the tars and their officers soon eased into friendly relations with the Maoris. Cook goes on:

> The advantage we received from the Natives coming to live by us was not a little. For some of them went out afishing every day when the weather would permit, and we generally got by exchanges a good part of the fruits of their labours... Besides the people who took up their abode by us, we were occasionally visited by others whose residence was not far off, and other who lived more remote. Their articles of commerce were, Curiosities, Fish and Women.[24]

'As an instance how much they trusted to our easiness,' wrote Lieutenant Burney, 'one man did not scruple to acknowledge his being present and assisting at the killing and eating the Adventures people.'[25] Burney, who was now serving as Clerke's second-in-command, watched the Maoris come and go:

> The Indians are about us, are in parties or Tribes seemingly unconnected with each other and live in different parts of Ship

---

[23] Ibid., p. 60.
[24] Ibid., p. 61.
[25] Burney, *Journey on HMS Discovery*, vol. 1, pp. 25-7.

Cove. One of these parties are accused by the rest of being the people who cutt off the Adventure's Boat. Their Chief whose Name is How-ura [*Kahura*] they say killed Rowe.[26]

February 14 saw the infamous warrior come to the *Resolution*, and cautiously seek a meeting with Cook. The navigator was away and missed him on this occasion. Cook recorded:

> Amongst these occasional Visitors was a Chief named Kahoura [*Kahura*], who headed the party that cut off Captain Furneaux's boat, and himself killed the officer that commanded. To judge of the character of this man by what some his Country said of him, he seemed to be a man more feared than beloved by them: many of them said he was a very bad man and importuned me to kill him, and I beleive they were not a little surprized that I did not, for accord[ing] to their ideas of equity this ought to have been done.[27]

The astronomer William Bayly, who spent that day assisting Cook, adds the natives were evasive when asked about Furneaux's men: 'By means of Omi [*Omai*] we endeavoured to learn the circumstances relative to our People being Kill'd last Voyage. They give us two accts.'[28]

Two days later, on February 16, Cook enticed a trusted Maori into discussing the massacre. The navigator had taken the five rowboats along the Sound to gather feed for the ships' cattle, and came near an infamous beach:

> we next proceeded down Grass Cove, remarkable for being the place where the Natives cut off Captain Furneaux's boat; here I met with my old friend Pedro [chief Matahoua], who was almost continually with me the last time I was in this Sound; he and another man received us on the beach, armed with the Pattoo [patu club] and spear, whether out of courtesy or of caution I cannot say; but I thought they shewed fear. However if they had any, a few presents soon removed them, and brought down [to

---

[26] Burney, *Journey on HMS Discovery*, vol. 1, p. 24.
[27] Beaglehole, *Journals of Cook*, vol. 3, pt. 1, p. 61.
[28] Robert McNab ed., *Historical Records of New Zealand*, John Mackay, Wellington, 1914, vol. 2, pp. 219-20.

the beach] two or three more of the family, but the greatest part of them remained out of sight.[29]

Whilst we were at this place, our curiosity prompt[ed] us to enquire the reason why our countrymen were killed; and Omai put several questions to Pedro and those about him on that head, all of which they answered without reserve, and like people who are under no apprehension of punishment for a crime they are not guilty of, for we already knew that none of these people had any hand in this unhappy affair...[30]

Showing Cook where the fight occurred, the Maoris described mistreatment by Furneaux's sailors in the days beforehand. Midshipman Rowe was key antagonist in a pattern of rough behaviour toward natives. Sometimes food and native artefacts offered in trade had been taken but naught given in return. The fatal clash with the foraging party came when the sailors were sitting down sharing food with Maoris. A theft was attempted, which lead to a scuffle where Rowe struck at Kahura with his hanger. The bleeding warrior then lead the massacre.[31]

Other Maoris volunteered similar information to Cook in following days. Given so many corroborating accounts, he did not doubt the truth of what they said. 'All agree,' he wrote,

> that the thing was not premeditated... For Kahoura's greatest enemies, those who solicited his distruction the most, owned that he had no intention to quarrel, much less to kill till the quarrell was actually commenced. It also appears that the unhappy Victims were under no sort of apprehension of their impending fate; otherwise they never would have sat down to a repast so far from thier boat, amongst people who the next Moment were to be their butcherers.[32]

---

[29] Beaglehole, *Journals of Cook*, vol. 3, pt. 1, p. 63.
[30] Ibid.
[31] J.C. Beaglehole, *The journals of Captain James Cook*, Hakluyt Society, Cambridge, 1971, vol. 4, pp. 521-2.
[32] Beaglehole, *Journals of Cook*, vol. 3, pt. 1, p. 64. Beaglehole suggests the requests for vengeance were probably because not long before Cook's arrival at the sound, more than seventy Maoris had been killed in a large tribal fight. Beaglehole, *Journals of Cook*, vol. 4, p. 522.

On February 24, the last day of the ships' stopover, a group of Maori men bearing articles for trade paddled up to the *Resolution* in large canoes.[33] Among them was Kahura, who, as his kinsmen bartered native dogs and carved Tikis for European hatchets, requested a meeting with the captain. The Tahitian translator Omai escorted him into the great cabin where all eyes fixed on the athletic Maori. 'He is a middle aged Man, very strong, & of a fierce Countenance tattowed after the Manner of the Country' wrote the surgeon's mate, while Dr Anderson himself observed 'He is a stout active man and to appearance turbulent and mischievous, as all the inhabitants concurr'd in giving him a bad character.'[34]

Omai introduced the warrior to Cook with the declaration, 'There is Kahourah kill him!'[35] Ignoring this outburst, the navigator used the translator to interview Kahura:

> I desired him to ask the cheif why he had killed Captain Furneaux's people, at this Question, he folded his arms hung down his head and looked like one caught in a trap; And I firmly believe [he expected] every moment to be his last, but was no sooner assured of his safety than he became cheerfull, yet he did not seem willing to answer the question that had been put to him till I had again and again assured him that he should not be hurt. Then he ventured to till us…[36]

Kahura's words tallied with what Cook had heard from others. Showing the scar he had from Rowe's blade, Kahura admitted leading the fight against the sailors which got out of hand, and afterward how he conducted a cannibal ceremony. Kahura extolled the sailors for fighting well, shooting two of his warriors dead before being overwhelmed. He also related how Burney's search party arrived the next day and their reaction at finding natives

---

[33] Beaglehole, *Journals of Cook*, vol. 3, pt. 2, pp. 818 & 1001.
[34] Ibid., pp. 818 & 998.
[35] Beaglehole, *Journals of Cook*, vol. 3, pt. 1, p. 64.
[36] Ibid.

consuming remains of the missing men.³⁷ The chief added that no Maoris were hurt when Burney ordered his marines to fire.

Kahura had now approached the *Resolution* three times, and a decision was needed. No directive on what to do if the navigator should meet the Maori killers was given in his 'secret instructions' for the expedition.³⁸ He accepted the fight had been largely of Rowe's own making, and it is evident Cook thought that at this late stage an execution would serve no constructive purpose.³⁹ So Cook publicly declared he forgave the warrior.⁴⁰

The Maoris' probably neither understood nor respected this act of leniency. From their perspective, to kill and ritually eat others harms the *mana* of their living kinfolk, and whether they inhabit the world securely. So when Kahura cut the sailors' hearts and heads from their bodies and, treating them as warrior rivals, ate them in the potent *wangai hau* ceremony, he stripped Cook and all his crew of ancestral protection.⁴¹ Maoris therefore expected lethal retribution; 'many of them seemed not only to wish it but surprized I did not,' Cook wrote, while Dr Anderson likewise noted 'several requested we would kill him [Kahura].'⁴² A grave wrong had occurred and, to native eyes, nothing less than execution would set matters right. The opinion of the many was expressed that day by the Tahitian aboard, Omai:

> seeing the chief unhurt, said "why do you not kill him, you till me if a man kills another in England he is hanged for it, this

---

³⁷ Ibid., pp. 64-5.
³⁸ Robert McNab ed., *Historical Records of New Zealand*, John Mackay, Wellington, 1914, Vol. 1, p. 24.
³⁹ Orchiston & Horrocks, 'Contact and Conflict,' op.cit., p. 533. The authors assess that at this time (Febrary 1777) Kahura's group comprised somewhere between sixty and a hundred people. (p. 536).
⁴⁰ Cook had undoubtedly discussed with Lords Sandwich and Morton, and others in London, the possibility of his encountering Kahura when he returned to New Zealand. But there is no written record of such conversations.
⁴¹ Anne Salmond, *Trial of the Cannibal Dog: Captain Cook in the South Seas*, Allen Lane, London, 2003, pp. 3-4.
⁴² Beaglehole, *Journals of Cook*, vol. 3, pt. 1, pp. 64-5; Beaglehole, *Journals of Cook*, vol. 3, pt. 2, p. 818.

Man has killed ten and yet you will not kill him, tho a great many of his countrymen desire it and it would be very good."[43]

So, then and there, the navigator set all to rest with an extraordinary gesture. Kahura had seen and admired a portrait of a Maori displayed in the great cabin. Cook suggested Kahura sit in the cabin and allow the expedition's artist, John Webber, to make a portrait of him in pen and ink. This was a signal honour, and its symbolism was equally understood by crewmen and natives. The chief solemnly agreed:

> [Kahura] sat till Mr Webber had finished it without the least restraint. I must confess I admired his courage and was not a little pleased at the confidence he put in me. Perhaps in this he placed his whole safety, for I had always declared to those who solicited his death that I had always been a friend to them all and would continue so unless they gave me cause to act otherwise; as to what was past, I should think no more of it as it was some time sence and done when I was not there…[44]

With this portrait, James Cook silenced further talk of the massacre in Queen Charlotte Sound. All knew that, for him, the subject was closed.

Webber's original portrait of Kahura is now in the Dixson Collection at the State Library of NSW, Sydney.[45] Made in pen and ink with touches of watercolour, the likeness is on a sheet of paper trimmed to measure 17¼ x 12½ in (43.8 x 31.3 cm). It shows the warrior's head and shoulders turned so he looks to the left. He wears a *pake pake* cloak, ear pendants of deep green New Zealand jade, his hair combed into a top-knot with four upright feathers.[46] The bearded Kahura has tattoos curling down from his

---

[43] Beaglehole, *Journals of Cook*, vol. 3, pt. 1, p. 68.
[44] Ibid., p. 69.
[45] Ref: DL Pe214, Dixson Library, State Library of New South Wales; Rüdiger Joppien and Bernard Smith, *The Art of Captain Cook's Voyages*, Oxford University Press, Sydney, New Haven and London, 1985-7, vol. 3, p. 284., cat.3.22. Webber also worked up an oil portrait from this, since lost. Bernard Smith, *Imagining the Pacific: In the Wake of the Cook Voyages*, Melbourne University Press, Melbourne, 1992, p.211 and note.
[46] Joppien & Smith, *Art of Captain Cook's Voyages*, vol. 3, p. 19.

left forehead into twisting whorls upon his nose which then flow back across his left cheek.

More than sixty of Webber's works made during the voyage became illustrations in the Atlas published as the official account of the third scientific expedition. Despite the care taken with Kahura's portrait, it was not selected for engraving as one of those plates. Yet a figure resembling him appears adjacent to Cook within one of Webber's large careful compositions portraying normal Maori life in New Zealand. Showing natives going about typical activities, the painting straddles the expedition's ethnographic aims and the political climate.

Considerable scientific advances across many fields were made on each of James Cook's voyages, but an ongoing popular fixation with Joseph Banks, that unstoppable self-promoter, has blurred shifting emphases. The first expedition was the botanical voyage, the second was the meteorological voyage, while the third was the ethnographic voyage.[47] We can see this in the immense body of visual art produced on the expeditions. The ethnographic material and landscape studies alone fill three sizable volumes in the illustrated catalogue published by the scholars Rüdiger Joppien and Bernard Smith over 1985-87.[48]

As for personnel who made this visual record, Sydney Parkinson (twenty-three years of age) on the first expedition was a talented botanical draftsman; William Hodges (twenty-eight) on the second expedition, former pupil of the landscapist Richard Wilson, was selected to record climatic differences and specifics of weather, particularly regional light; while John Webber (twenty-four) on the third expedition, who was adept at illustrating rustic life, put a capable hand to representing anything rural: animals, plants, natural settings, unlikely dwellings, country folk in ethnic

---

[47] Smith, *European Vision*, chs. 2, 3 & 4; also Smith, *Imagining the Pacific*, p. 193.
[48] Joppien & Smith, *Art of Captain Cook's Voyages*. There is a volume for each of Cook's Pacific voyages, although volume three physically comprises two thick volumes.

costume.[49] There was also on the *Endeavour* expedition Alexander Buchan who was to draw landscapes and natives; but, an epileptic, he tragically died four days after arriving in Tahiti. (After Buchan died Solander's assistant from the British Museum, Herman Spöring, took down drawings of native artefacts and landscapes.[50]) And also William Ellis, surgeon's second mate on the *Discovery*, acted as natural history draughtsman on the last voyage.

If each of these professionals was intermittently called to work outside their specialisation, with mixed results, they were chiefly to observe and scientifically record in line with their skills. Parkinson assisted the Linnean botanists Dr Daniel Solander and Joseph Banks. Despite expiring of dysentery late in the *Endeavour* expedition, Parkinson's 955 botanical drawings made in the Pacific are deservedly much known, with his forensic depictions of plants setting a benchmark for later taxonomic art.

Hodges worked on the *Adventure* under the naturalists Johann and Georg Forster—and to a lesser degree the astronomers William Wales[51] and William Bayly—producing landscapes which

---

[49] For an overview of Webber's oeuvre, see William Hauptman curator, *John Webber 1751-1793: Landschaftsmaler und Südseefahrer/ Pacific Voyager and Landscape Artist*, Kunstmuseum Bern, 1996.

[50] Herman Spöring was aboard the *Endeavour* as an assistant naturalist, and, carrying a set of watchmaker's tools, maintained the expedition's scientific instruments. If he had completed studies in medicine and surgery in Åbo then Stockholm, Spöring had initially worked as a watchmaker when he settled in London. After apparently meeting Solander through the Swedish Church, he joined the British Museum as an assistant, helping Solander sort the botanical component of the natural history collection into Lineaen order. Spöring's technically-oriented drawings reveal a fascination with intricate interlocking geometric forms, as evident in a sequence of meticulous studies of Maori carvings. Edward Duyker, *Nature's Argonaut: Daniel Solander 1733-1782*, Melbourne University Press, Melbourne, 1998, p. 81.

[51] In 1775, not long after the completion of the Pacific voyage, William Wales was appointed Master of Mathematics at Christ's Hospital School, London. A popular teacher, he would intermittently relate to pupils some of his experiences on Cook's expedition. The students included Samuel Taylor Coleridge, who from the ages of fifteen to nineteen was taught by Wales. Working with Wales's own journal from the voyage, Bernard Smith has been able to identify events on the second expedition that seemingly later inspired portions of Coleridge's major poem *The Rime of the Ancyent Marinere* (1798). See "Coleridge's Ancient Mariner and Cook's Second Voyage", in Smith, *Imagining the Pacific*, ch.6. (cf. Richard Holmes, *Coleridge: Early Visions*, Hodder & Stoughton, London, 1989, pp. 140, 173n.)

prompted a transformation in geographic understanding. They were intently studied by the young Alexander von Humboldt, being a formative influence upon his researches into the earth's climactic zones. Those visual studies not only mark the threshold to climate science; they spurred the shift in British landscape art away from formulaic Italianate scenery to observational views which conveyed the geographic character of place and its local light.[52] Cotman, Constable and their followers would have been very different painters if not for Hodges's scientifically informed work in the Pacific.

John Webber, the third artist, answered to James Cook. There were surely occasions when instructions were given by the *Resolution*'s surgeon William Anderson, who doubled as the expedition's naturalist; but Cook was boss. The navigator had clear expectations of what he wanted from an artist.[53] He was more than ever aware that he was making contemporary history, and he was already planning a book on the third expedition before leaving London.[54] Distilled from his twelve years of exploration, this would be Cook's authorative statement on the Pacific and its diverse peoples, a response to Charles de Brosses, and a corrective to John Hawkesworth.[55] For it he needed an accurate visual record of natives and their daily life for use as illustrations. Daniel Solander recommended Webber to him.

The artists on all three expeditions made detailed drawings of native utensils, tools, musical instruments, weapons, fishing

---

[52] Joppien & Smith, *Art of Captain Cook's Voyages*, vol. 2; Smith, *Imagining the Pacific*, ch .5.

[53] Smith, *Imagining the Pacific*, p. 73.

[54] Ibid., pp. 73, 181.

[55] James Cook owned a copy of Charles de Brosses's *Histoire des Navigations aux Terres Australes* (1756) which he consulted intermittently on his voyages, checking information on Dutch and Hispanic explorers. Joseph Banks also had a copy among the books he carried on the *Endeavour*. De Brosses's *Histoire* was a compendium of all known voyages in the South Seas. The author urged future navigators heading for the Pacific to take along natural historians and scientific illustrators to gather information. It was due to de Brosses that the geographic terms 'Polynesia' and 'Australia' gained broad use in the late 18th century.

equipment, clothing, ornaments, tattoos, canoes and dwellings. What sets Webber apart is how, during the expedition, he used ethnographic information gathered in the field to work up paintings portraying the different Pacific peoples on location: Tasmanian Aboriginals, New Zealand Maori, Polynesians in Tonga, Tahiti and Hawaii, Canadian Indians, Siberian Chukchi. In *Imagining the Pacific* (1992), his watershed study of how Cook's voyages reshaped European thought, Bernard Smith points out

> No other artist before had been called upon to draw so many varied ethnic types. [Webber] is Europe's first serious ethnographic artist and his work stands on the threshold of ethnography as science. It was his business not only to draw native peoples as such but also to distinguish as best he could the visual differences to be observed between one ethnic group and another. He was the first artist to make Europeans aware of the great variety of peoples who inhabited the Pacific.[56]

In ink and watercolour, those paintings show natives undertaking group activities, including fishing, hunting, cooking, using canoes, exercising, wrestling, making music, dancing, performing rituals and, of course, meeting the European explorers. There is a significant omission: apart from his renowned picture *The Death of Cook*, the illustrations devised by the artist do not have native peoples involved in violence or hostilities. 'Webber's developed compositions constructed on the voyage and for the official publication seem to be saying the same thing,' Smith continues. 'The people of the Pacific are indeed pacific people.'[57]

Most telling is the composition *Captain Cook in Ship Cove, Queen Charlotte Sound* of 1777. Now in London's National Maritime Museum, the original is in pen and watercolour on a large sheet of paper measuring 24 x 38½ in (60.7 x 98.5 cm).[58] Webber made it aboard ship under Cook's supervision. The artist

---

[56] Smith, *Imagining the Pacific*, p. 181.
[57] Ibid., p. 199.
[58] Joppien & Smith, *Art of Captain Cook's Voyages*, vol. 3, p. 276, cat.3.14.

used part of the *Resolution*'s cabin as a shared workspace with William Bligh, the expedition's cartographer. So Anderson, Clerke and Bligh would also have seen Webber develop the composition, probably giving feedback.

Captain Cook in Ship Cove, Queen Charlotte Sound shows a tranquil scene where New Zealand natives go about daily activities in a small village before thick forest. Twenty-two Maori figures of different ages appear in the composition. The right quarter of the picture opens out to a view of a sandy beach with the *Discovery* and *Resolution* at anchor in the distance. We see sailors tending the jolly boat at the shore, while Captain Cook is standing up a gentle slope at the edge of the village, shaking hands with a lean older Maori probably modelled on Matahoua (Cook's friend 'Pedro'). Two Europeans, presumably Clerke and Anderson, accompany Cook while just to the right of them a muscular Maori in a feathered cloak, whose head resembles Kahura, is bearing a *taiaha* and walking from several beached canoes toward the native huts.

This scene is a fiction.[59] It is not what occurred when Cook returned to the bay. His journal describes local Maoris as initially cautious about approaching Europeans when the ships had appeared. And the Maori dwellings on the foreshore were erected once cordial relations were re-established. Besides, Cook and Webber knew *hongi*, rubbing noses, was the method of formal greeting among Maoris, using this on expeditions, not handshakes.[60]

Why then does the picture depart so significantly from truth? Bernard Smith suggests more than idealisation is involved: 'Ethnographical information of great interest is being conveyed about the nature of the temporary habitations, the dress and adornment of the Maori, but it is conveyed within the framework

---

[59] Joppien and Smith describe the work as 'one of those 'history' drawings that document events of the expedition in a narrative manner. Cook, the peaceful hero, the pacifier of South Sea nations, has gone on to establish good relations with those people on whose food supplies the fate of the expedition so much depended.' Joppien & Smith, *Art of Captain Cook's Voyages*, vol. 3, p 18.

[60] Salmond, *Trial of the Cannibal Dog*, p. 117.

of a potentially political message: Cook the friendly voyager meeting his old friends the Maori.'[61] The picture also resolves a troubling matter, given the depicted scene is near where Furneaux's men were notoriously massacred then eaten by Kahura's warriors. What Webber contrived is the image of an abundant, supportive land where Maori and European henceforth interact in friendship and concord. Peace now reigns.

How the British government used its navy overseas was a sensitive subject in the early 1770s. The political climate was positively turbulent as the American colonies agitated over parliamentary representation. The matter wouldn't rest.

London was chewing on this deteriorating colonial situation when the *Adventure* sailed alone back along the south coast during 1774. Furneaux may have quit the Pacific mission before completion. He may also have lost ten crew members to cannibals. Yet he carried on board Omai, a native youth from the far side of the world.[62] Taken under the wings of Joseph Banks and the Earl of Sandwich, the Tahitian was presented to the King and Queen, dined with fellows of the Royal Society, was paraded before Dukes and Bishops, posed for a flamboyant portrait by Sir Joshua Reynolds, toured the counties with landed gentry, rode in a fox hunt, went to a race meeting, to the opera, to musical recitals, to preening parties in the Vauxhall Gardens.[63]

---

[61] Smith, *Imagining the Pacific*, op.cit., p.204; cf. Joppien & Smith, *Art of Captain Cook's Voyages*, vol. 3, p. 17.

[62] Furneaux had entered Omai in his ship's muster book as 'Tetuby Homey' from Huahine, Society Islands, '22 years, Able Seaman.' Richard Holmes, *The Age of Wonder: How the Romantic Generation Discovered the Beauty and Terror of Science*, HarperPress, London, 2008, p. 49.

[63] Willam Hodges made an oil sketch of Omai from life for the surgeon John Hunter (it is now in collection of the Royal College of Surgeons) which seems the more accurate portrayal of the Tahitian we have. In comparison, Joshua Reynolds made a flattering observational drawing of Omai, followed this with a stagey oil portrait which treats the Polynesian as a blend of Roman senator and Indian maharajah.. So there was, as Bernard Smith observes, a tension between the claims of science and the claims of artistic taste. See Smith, *Imagining the Pacific*, p. 175; Smith, *European Vision*, pp. 80-2, illus. pl.12; also E.H.McCormick, *Omai, Pacific Envoy*, Auckland University Press, Auckland, 1977, p. 174.

Fashionable society was abuzz, jostling to meet the authentic noble savage as Mr Banks and Lord Sandwich steered their trophy on a circuit of select introductions: 'He had on a suit of Manchester velvet,' noted Fanny Burney, 'Lined with lace satten, a Bag, lace Ruffles, & a very handsome sword which the King had given him... Omai appears in a new world like a man [who] had all his life studied the Graces.' His hands, she added, were 'very much tatooed, but his face is not at all. He is by no means handsome, though I like his countenance.'[64]

Some viewed the Polynesian as a test case for civilised improvement.[65] He was taught to play chess, to saddle a horse, to dance like a European gentleman, and offered long-winded counsel on how to advance agriculture when he returned to the South Seas. His popularity could not seem higher when, during May 1775, the Royal Academy's spring exhibition opened in Pall Mall. Visitors found Reynold's just finished painting of Omai paired on the wall with a new portrait of that avatar of rank and fashion, Georgiana, the Duchess of Devonshire.[66]

Omai, a common Tahitian without tribal status, relished the attention. But his stagey bows, fractured English, forced manners and social gaffes—he greeted George III with the words 'How do King Tosh!'[67]—saw him viewed in some quarters as a target for cruel fun. The grinning native was merging right into 'only the best company,' quipped Samuel Johnson, becoming so like the Irish *macaroni* Lord Mulgrave 'that I was afraid to speak to

---

[64] Charlotte Barrett ed. *The Diary and Letters of Madame d'Arblay (Fanny Burney)*, Hurst & Blackett, London, 1854, vol. 1, p. 370; Peter McNeill, *Pretty Gentlemen: Macaroni Men and the Eighteenth Century Fashion World*, Yale University Press, New Haven, 2018, p. 97; Rickard, *Sailing with Cook*, op.cit., p.186. When they reached Britain, Omai spent time with Lieutenant James Burney's family, staying with his father and sister, the musicologist Dr Charles Burney and writer Fanny Burney.
[65] Roy Porter, *Enlightenment: Britain and the Creation of the Modern World*, Allen Lane, London, 2000, p. 361.
[66] McCormick, *Omai, Pacific Envoy*, p. 174.
[67] Holmes, *Age of Wonder*, pp. 51-2.

either, lest I should mistake one for the other.'[68] Tellingly, Joseph Banks dropped Omai.

Then came a stinging broadside. It took the form of a fictional letter written in heroic couplets by an anonymous agitator, and which appeared in print during June 1775. With an eye on the writings of Alexander Pope and Jonathan Swift, *An Historical Epistle from Omiah to the Queen of Otaheite, being his Remarks on the English Nation* followed in that Augustan tradition of planting sharp political criticism within literary satire. In deftly crafted verse a guileless traveller reports, like Lemuel Gulliver, upon the wonders he has witnessed in a strange land. This visitor is no less than Omai the Tahitian, and his letter about England—which intermittently borrows from complaints of American colonists—is unsparing in its portrayal of a smug avarice:

> Can Europe boast, with all her pilfer'd wealth,
> A larger store of happiness, or health?
> What then avail her thousand arts to gain
> The store of every land and every main:
> Whilst we, whom love's more grateful joys enthrall,
> Profess one art—to live without them all.[69]

Parliamentarians, the clergy, polite society are all targeted for mockery; and the writer takes a firm crack at a tangled, self-serving legal system ('Not rul'd like us on nature's simple plan,/ Here laws on laws perplex the dubious man.'). Especially biting is a passage where, invoking both new voyages of exploration and the ongoing slave trade, the Tahitian complains of purportedly high-minded nations which:

> ... in cool blood premeditately go
> To murder wretches whom they cannot know,

---

[68] Boswell, *Life of Johnson*, p. 723; see also 608; McCormick, *Omai, Pacific Envoy*, p. 169. Within his circle of friends, Johnson referred to Baron Mulgrave as "the blockhead".

[69] McCormick, *Omai, Pacific Envoy*, pp. 142-4; Smith, *Imagining the Pacific*, p. 202.

Urg'd by no injury, prompted by no ill
In forms they butcher, and by systems kill;
Cross o'er the seas, to ravage distant realms,
And ruin thousands worthier than themselves.[70]

An Historical Epistle from Omiah was among a run of literary works on the South Seas that appeared in the 1770s, most evoking an idyllic Golden Age, some satirically barbed.[71] Denis Diderot even dabbled with this in his *Supplément au voyage de Bougainville* (1772), the supposed reflections of an old Tahitian distressed by French explorers. Yet in its cutting criticism of Georgian Britain, and suggestions of brutalities inflicted upon native populations, *An Historical Epistle from Omiah* was certainly noticed. James Cook was reputedly shown the mocking verse when he got back from the Pacific in July. And Lord Sandwich, the head of the navy, began to view Omai as a political embarrassment.[72]

This begs the question of how naval vessels were to function in the South Seas. Among the orders the Admiralty gave Cook when the *Endeavour* had departed for Tahiti was a section on his conduct toward natives—a paragraph repeated in the Admiralty's orders for his subsequent two Pacific expeditions. It ran, in full:

> You are likewise to observe the Genius, Temper, Disposition, and Number of the Natives and Inhabitants, where you find any; and to endeavour, by all proper means to cultivate a friendship with them; making them Presents of such Trinkets as you may have on board, and they may like best; inviting them to Traffick; and shewing them every Civility and Regard;

---

[70] McCormick, *Omai, Pacific Envoy*, p. 143; Smith, *Imagining the Pacific*, p. 202.

[71] The playfully cheeky, if anonymous *Transmigration* of 1778, wonders about the sexual exploits of Banks and Solander in Tahiti. See Smith, *European Vision and the South Pacific*, pp. 46-51.

[72] Casting the Tahitian as a noble savage, both Salmond's and Holmes's accounts of Omai in London are most positive and omit negative voices. However, it is apparent Omai had become a political embarrassment after eighteen months and Lord Sandwich wanted him returned to Tahiti. Salmond, *Trial of the Cannibal Dog*, p.293-302; Holmes, *Age of Wonder*, pp. 49-51.

but taking care nevertheless not to suffer yourself to be surprised by them...[73]

The president of the Royal Society and renowned Scottish astronomer James Douglas, the fourteenth Earl of Morton, also prepared a memorandum advising Cook on aspects of the *Endeavour* voyage. The Society was the sponsor for this pioneering scientific expedition, and the document embodied the ideals of the philosophers of the Enlightenment. For example, the instructions on how Cook should treat natives suggests the Royal Society considered Pacific exploration as a step toward building a universal brotherhood of mankind lead by Europeans—this memorandum appears an early motivation for the overt fraternal tenor of the compositions made by John Webber, under Cook's supervision, on the third Pacific expedition.[74]

On hostile actions or violence from natives, Lord Morton advised:

> Have it still in view that shedding the blood of those people is a crime of the highest nature:- They are human creatures, the work of the same omnipotent Author, under his care with the most polished European; perhaps less offensive, more entitled to favour... Therefore should they in a hostile manner oppose a landing, and kill some men in the attempt, even this would hardly justify firing among them, till every other gentle method had been tried. There are many ways to convince them of the Superiority of Europeans.[75]

Lofty principles may have sat well in the Royal Society's rooms off Fleet Street, but how to apply them in the field? On his expeditions Cook did not go out of his way to connect with unknown native communities. His journals indicate when people on land and huts were sighted as his ship sailed along a coastline; and serious attention was given to smoke ashore as it indicated

---

[73] Quoted in Smith, *Imagining the Pacific*, p. 197.
[74] Ibid., pp. 207-8.
[75] Quoted in Ibid., p. 207.

how densely an area was populated. But there was no automatic attempt to stop and parley with natives. Landfall occurred as needed. This was to obtain fresh water, food for his crew, fodder for the ship's livestock, and to undertake nautical maintenance. Frequent landings were unnecessary. It was a need for water that forced the stop at Botany Bay

Still, Naval orders and Lord Morton's instructions were clearly converted into working methods used when dealing with Pacific natives. Cook was cautious if unknown groups and native crowds approached shore parties, as well as strangers in canoes paddling to his ship. Then come instances of armed hostility where natives threaten sailors with clubs or pikes, or hurl rocks, 'darts' or spears. When a situation becomes dangerous a defensive shot is fired in the air above the natives. With those in watercraft, failure to move off led to shots aimed at the canoe's hull, affecting its buoyancy; while for shore encounters, small shot to 'sting' them was fired at aggressors who didn't withdraw (the equivalent of rubber bullets today).

The rule was defend with minimal response, aiming to cause least injury. Where light shot did not repel hostile strangers on shore, as last resort Cook had marines use bullets, targeting a main aggressor. The journals of ships' officers and other travellers on Cook's voyages verify this, confirming that lives had to be in direct peril before he authorised shooting at a native. For example, shots were used defensively to scare or wound on the two occasions Australian Aboriginals were fired upon. In the first instance (Apr. 1770) spears were hurled at Europeans when they landed at Botany Bay, and in the second (July 1770) a native set a grass fire and seemingly tried to burn out the ship's camp by the Endeavour River.[76] Cook ordered restraint and no native was killed on either occasion. Mind you, Johann and George Forster, the naturalists on the second expedition, were later critical of

---

[76] Notably, Joseph Banks had warned Cook at Botany Bay that Aboriginal spears were potentially poisoned, although this did not prompt him to resort to greater force.

this practice, believing it too easily lead to bloodshed (although Johann himself was quick with his trigger finger). Excited natives greeting Cook might mistakenly be fired on. But it was by using firearms that Tiata, a Tahitian youth travelling on the *Endeavour*, was rescued when Maori warriors in a canoe grabbed and tried to make off with him.[77]

Defensive shots were usually followed by further efforts to negotiate. This could see Cook sometimes have the ship's surgeon treat their injuries, or compensate wounded natives—as happened at Tonga on the second expedition. Lieutenant Clerke had taken a party from the *Resolution* to obtain fresh water, and an affable native group mingled with the tars as barrels were filled. When they finished Clerke found thefts had occurred, including the surgeon's musket and the cooper's tools. So Cook came ashore and tried to parley a return of the equipment. After much fruitless negotiation, he called out his marines. He writes:

> At length the Marines arrived which gave them [the natives] some alarm in so much that some fled but I prevailed on the greatest part to stay; the first Step I took was to seize on two Large double Sailing Canoes which were in the Cove, one fellow making some resistance I fired at him with Small Shott which sent him limping off.[78]

The Tongans at once gave back the stolen items. By way of apology they also offered the expedition's leader a young woman, and were bewildered when he refused this gift. Actually, Cook was concerned about the native who had just been shot, asking to see him:

> the wound'd man was brought on a board and laid down at my feet ... tho he was wounded both in the hand and thigh neither

---

[77] Likewise Beaglehole records that firearms were required in the New Hebrides when Cook first landed in a launch. When he and his men tried to go back to the *Resolution* natives snatched away the oars from the beached rowboat, then threw stones and spears. One tar took a spear in his cheek. A shot was fired above the crowd whereupon, surprised by the percussive sound of gun powder, the natives released the launch. Beaglehole, *Journals of Cook*, vol. 4, p. 429.

[78] Beaglehole, *Journals of Cook*, vol. 2, p. 143. The incident was on June 28, 1774.

the one nor the other were dangerous. I however sent for the Surgeon a Shore to dress his wounds... When the Surgeon arrived he dress'd the mans wounds let him blood and was of opinion that he was in no sort of danger as the shott had done little more than penetrate the Skin.[79]

A poultice was applied to ensure the victim's full recovery, then Cook gave his family valued goods (a knife and an iron spike) as recompense for the incident.

Difficulties initiating trade recurred when ships halted at new locations. The Europeans were keen to purchase fresh fish, fruit and meat. But most Pacific cultures were unfamiliar with trade, so natives mistook efforts to barter for a presentation of gifts. It was common for early attempted swaps to end with a native taking the cloth on offer while smilingly keeping the item the sailor desired. Systems were developed. Realising how Islanders prized red feathers, Cook later used them for barter across Polynesia. And in Monuka, Tonga, he would establish a temporary marketplace on a beach. Otherwise the travellers found the west coast of Canada the only place where trade was known, Indians being within an extended fur trading network. On his third expedition, Cook was disconcerted at how Canadian Indians expected payment for anything taken. If firewood was gathered, fodder cut for the livestock, or fresh water taken from a creek, local natives wanted compensation.

Cook issued guidelines for trade. He formally read these rules aloud to his crew, saying they must 'endeavour by all proper means to cultivate a friendship with the Natives, by showing them every kind civility and regard.'[80] Officers supervised exchanges. Unauthorised barter incurred a flogging, as did trading supplies from the ships' stores, or swapping nails for anything other than fresh provisions. Animated arguments with a native might also

---

[79] Beaglehole, *Journals of Cook*, vol. 2, pp. 143-4.
[80] Cook's five articles governing trade between sailors and natives were taken down word for word by Lieutenant Burney. See Burney, Private Journal, 16 Aug. 1773, quoted in Rickard, *Sailing with Cook*, p. 123.

incur the cat. Cook abhorred any effort to trick or exploit natives; 'It has ever been a maxim with me to punish the least crimes of any of my people committed against these uncivilised Nations,' he wrote. 'Their robbing us with impunity is by no means a sufficient reason why we should treat them in the same manner...'[81] This is why Cook noted a violation of orders in the ship's journal when Lieutenant Gore shot at a native over a trade gone wrong, the navigator insisting [we] 'know how to Chastise Trifling faults like this without taking away their lives.'[82]

Cook had qualms about prostitution, realising women were often forced by male relatives or tribal chiefs to have sex with visitors. His crew was cleared of venereal diseases before leaving England, but sailors did pick up infections at Foreign ports and on Pacific islands. On the third voyage, after being alerted by Dr Anderson to several men contracting tropical yaws, Cook forbade them from further relations with native women. One tar disobeyed. He was humiliated, flogged, then confined to ship for its stay at the island.

There always were problems with theft in the South Seas. Polynesians tried to steal whatever took their fancy, from items of clothing to maritime hardware, even astronomer's instruments. Younger males treated theft as a sport, stealing metal buttons and buckles from marines who dozed off when standing guard on deck at night. Unidentified Tahitians prised nails out of ships' fittings on each visit there. All the officers became frustrated over thefts. When a Maori was caught making off with a half-hour glass timer used to calculate speed, filched from the helmsman's binnacle on the *Endeavour*, the alarmed ship's master Lieutenant Hicks had the offender flogged before tribe members. Thieving halted at that anchorage; but it had to be dealt with again at the next stopover.

---

[81] Beaglehole, *Journals of Cook*, vol. 2, p. 292.
[82] J.C. Beaglehole, (editor), *The Journals of Captain James Cook on His Voyages of Discovery, Vol.1: The Voyage of the* Endeavour *1768-1771*, Cambridge, at the University Press, for the Hakluyt Society, 1968, p. 196.

Cook accepted theft mostly with stoic resignation. On one occasion at Tahiti when he spent the night in a tent, the navigator placed his stockings beneath his pillow believing them secure under his head. Upon waking the next morning, Cook was amused to find his stockings gone. Yet there were occasions when he lost patience. Later on his last voyage—when he was suffering seriously deteriorating health—in desperation the navigator ordered hair and eyebrows shaved off Islanders caught stealing, then chunks sliced from their ears and lobes cut off. This shocked officers and regular sea hands, who worried their commander was behaving quite out of character. It didn't bring thefts to an end, either.

Cook and more alert crew members kept out of disputes between natives. Rival tribal figures tried to enlist the officers' support when Cook revisited Tahiti on his second expedition; and it was obvious power games were underway. Likewise Cook was careful in Hawaii, where he was taken for either a chieftan or a god. Any endorsement there would have potent cultural implications. Throughout Polynesia, the navigator rebuffed occasional requests for violent intervention. Seemingly peaceful natives would ask him to kill tribal adversaries. This was evidently distressing Cook on his final visit to Queen Charlotte Sound, the fifth time he had stopped there, when over ten days a sequence of affable Maoris pressed him to execute chief Kahura.[83] The navigator despairingly erupted in his journal:

> If I followed the advice of all our pretended friends I might have extirpated the whole race, for the people of each Hamlet or village by turns applyed to me to distroy the other, a very striking proof of the divided state in which they live.[84]

The peoples of New Zealand already had a reputation for aggression before Cook's arrival. Abel Tasman, the Dutch

---

[83] Cook had previously stopped at Queen Charlotte Sound in January 1770, May 1773, November 1773, and October 1774. Besides replenishing fresh water and food at the anchorage, he used the beach there to careen, scub and repair his vessels.

[84] Beaglehole, *Journals of Cook*, vol. 3, pt. 1, p. 62.

navigator who came upon the west coast in 1643, naming this new land after a province in the Netherlands, had tried to instigate trade. He sent a small boat to barter cloth and other merchandise with the natives on shore. A Maori war canoe rammed it and four of the sailors were clubbed to death. So Tasman had his two ships weigh anchor and leave without landing, whereupon eleven large native canoes crammed with warriors gave determined chase. Europeans henceforth avoided the islands for over a century.

Cook was determined to establish cordial relations with the Maori, although his initial efforts were a tragedy of misunderstandings. Natives were sighted soon after the *Endeavour* arrived at New Zealand in October 1769. Recognising them as armed warriors, the explorers were cautious; and firearms had to be resorted to several times in the first days.

On the second occasion, when Cook, Banks and Solander went ashore in the yawl, a Maori group appeared a short distance away and, waving clubs, performed a *haka*. There was no mistaking this as a war dance. Instead of withdrawing Cook signalled for the pinnace with a squad of marines. They arrived, accompanied by the translator Tupia, the ship's surgeon Dr Monkhouse, and the astronomer and mathematician Charles Green.[85] As a precaution against needless casualties, Cook allowed one marine to load his musket with ball, ordering the rest to load with light shot.[86] Words of greeting by Tupia saw thirty of the warriors move in close, although the Tahitian was apprehensive, warning Cook they were volatile. After accepting gifts offered, the natives tried to snatch away the Europeans' bladed weapons. One seized Green's hanger, wouldn't give it back, then other Maoris turned aggressive. The

---

[85] A civilian, Green was responsible for taking sightings of the sun, moon and planets then computing the Endeavour's exact position each day. This involved complex calculations and enabled Cook to map the ocean with a high degree of accuracy. The navigator mentions in his journal that Green had been training up the ship's petty officers (who then included Charles Clerke and Richard Pickersgill) to undertake this demanding work in future.

[86] J.C. Beaglehole, *The Endeavour Journal of Joseph Banks*, Angus & Robertson, Sydney, 1962, p. 402.

thief was shot, so the warriors rushed behind a rocky outcrop. Further efforts to parley were not tried.

That afternoon, when crossing a bay, Cook had his sailors row toward two native canoes, intending to come alongside and 'by good treatment and presents endeavour to gain their friendship.'[87] The Maoris paddled away. Cook relates: 'I order'd a Musquet to be fir'd over their Heads, thinking that this would either make them surrender or jump overboard; but here I was misstaken for they immidiately took to their arms or whatever they had in the boat and began to attack us.'[88] Guns were resorted to, three Maoris being killed, and another wounded: 'I am aware that most humane men who have not experienced things of this nature will censure my conduct...' runs Cook's troubled journal entry for October 10, 'nor do I myself think that the reason I had for seizing upon [the canoe] will at all justify me, and had I thought they would make the least resistance I would not have come near them.'[89]

Three youths tried to swim off, but the sailors pulled them from the water. The natives feared that the strangers were cannibals. Taken aboard the *Endeavour*, they were given gifts, clothing, food, 'and to the surprise of every body became at once as cheerful and as merry as if they had been with their own friends.'[90] This meeting proved decisive as word would spread of how kindly the trio was treated.

The youths pleaded not to be put ashore the following morning, saying warriors nearby might kill and eat them. Cook was sceptical; although cannibalism came up in conversation with other Maori groups encountered as the *Endeavour* moved along the coast. Then, near Waikawa Bay, Cook and Banks met

---

[87] Beaglehole, *Journals of Cook,* vol. 1, p. 170.
[88] Ibid.
[89] Beaglehole, *Journals of Cook,* vol. 1, p. 171; in his own journal, Banks recorded this as "the most disagreeable day My life has yet seen, black be the mark for it and heaven send that such may never return to embitter future reflection." Joseph Banks, *The Endeavour Journal of Sir Joseph Banks*, State Library of NSW, Vol. 1, entry for 14 April 1769.
[90] Beaglehole, *Journals of Cook,* vol. 1, p. 171.

with warriors who boasted of having just eaten enemies, showing them the bone from a forearm. That afternoon more natives approached in a canoe, including a woman with heavily scarred arms and thighs. It was explained she had done this to mourn her deceased husband, a victim of cannibalism. Two days later a shore party came upon gnawed human bones at a Maori fireplace. Next morning warriors paddled up in a canoe with four fresh heads of men they had killed and consumed, Banks obtaining one head in a barter. Then, on 30 January 1770, Cook watched as five newly widowed women scarred their own limbs—a customary mourning ritual when husbands were eaten by warrior rivals.

Back in London there was consternation when Cook and Banks recounted these incidents. Cannibalism did not fit with Europeans' idealistic beliefs about Pacific peoples. But on Cook's next expedition the ship's officers found the butchered corpse of a youth on a beach in Queen Charlotte Sound. Maoris had even fixed its raw heart to a canoe's prow. Lieutenant Pickersgill purchased the corpse's head from a warrior for two nails, and brought it back to the *Resolution* intending to take it to Britain as a scientific specimen. Then a native came aboard, saw the head, and there was gesturing; so Lieutenant Clerke cut away a severed flap of cheek dangling off, roasted it using the galley's grill, and the Maori avidly devoured the flesh. Cook suggested they offer him the entire head if cooked, which was done, and warrior consumed all. This unsettled the tars, some deckhands vomiting, while the shocked Tahitian interpreter Oedidee rebuked the Maori for the practice. Cook noted all in his journal for the sake of doubters. Cannibalism was now confirmed—little did he suspect that four weeks later ten crew from his expedition's second vessel, the *Adventure*, would be massacred and eaten by warriors nearby.

Perceptions of James Cook are impeded by two competing cliches: the British worthy, and the evil white man. Each is a rhetorical trope employed for argument's sake, although by converting this individual into a cultural abstraction they omit revealing facts.

Like his ethnic identity, which had implications in a nation fixated with rank. Raised in the remote and rural North Riding, James Cook spoke with a pronounced Yorkshire accent. He also seems to have retained a Northern vocabulary; so where most naval officers he mixed with used words like *small*, *girl* and *children*, he would have said *wee*, *lass* and *bairns*. Its also likely that during youth he was called 'Jamie' in his Northern community, not the 'Jack' or 'Jim' used in the South. This may strike some as inconsequential, but it was significant. Being from the Northern counties carried a stigma in Georgian Britain. To some extent it still does.

Young James was the second son of James Cook, a rural day labourer, and his wife Grace. They lived in a two room thatched cottage at Marton-in-Cleveland, a hamlet overlooking the Tees River, about twelve miles upstream from the North Sea. Raising a family was a struggle. Not counting miscarriages, Grace Cook bore eight children, although five died in infancy or youth. James would be the sole surviving son. Childhood for this skinny red-haired youngster was circumscribed by the seasonal routines of beasts, crops and land. The family moved twice, both to slightly better cottages, which were surely linked with Cook senior advancing to better agricultural jobs. Then he was appointed a 'hind' or farm foreman—indicating he could read and write—upon which the eleven-year-old James, who already knew his alphabet, was enrolled in the village school at Great Ayton. There the lad learnt the elements of reading, writing and arithmetic. What would be useful, not a scrap more; yet they were valued skills, and enabled this determined farm-boy later to teach himself much, rising from a humble background.[91]

---

[91] Geoffrey Blainey attributes Cook's attitude to learning and self improvement to his Scottish enthnicity. Geoffrey Blainey, *Captain Cook's Epic Voyage: The Strange Quest for a Missing Continent*, Penguin, Melbourne, 2020, pp. 4-5.

Features we associate with a privileged officer class are missing from this upbringing. Creature comforts were outside Cook's experience; nor did he acquire Latin, Greek and that fluency in the Classics expected of future leaders and polished sophisticates. This surely explains the matter-of-factness to how he later wrote his journals, the direct prose, as well as the names he gave islands, hills, bays and straits.[92] Cook never used Classical phrases. Where a Louis de Bougainville might flamboyantly call an island *La nouvelle Cythera*, invoking the mythical isle of love, in contrast Cook gave formal dedications (Cape Moreton), rewarded his crew (Pickersgill Island), applied visual resemblance (Mount Dromedary), marked incidents (Kidnappers Bay), or invoked the home country (New Caledonia).

At sixteen years of age James was apprenticed at a haberdashers-cum-grocery store in Staithes, a fishing village fifteen miles south. Shop assistant was a step up for the entire family, a move away from rural labour. The lad's change in circumstances coincided with events that would, at the very least, have concerned his father.

Ethnicity plays a role here, because Cook senior was a lowland Scot. He was born and raised within a sheep farming community near Kelso in the Tweed Dale. But he had left the border country and travelled along the coast to North Yorkshire in 1715. This corresponded with a Jacobite uprising when, after years of tension, the British throne passed to George of Hanover. Many Scots relocated after the rebels were defeated that year. They had to, given an adverse social and political climate. Worst affected were the rural poor, who could be abruptly displaced upon the seizure of a Jacobite laird's property. Even language was affected. 'Tory' from the Gaelic market insult *torai* (robber), and 'Whig' from *whiggamore* (cattle driver), which both had recently drifted into parliamentary slang, now became embedded in common English.

---

[92] In the introduction to his book on his second Pacific voyage, Cook requested the reader excuse "inaccuracies of Style" because his prose is "the production of a man who has been constantly at sea from his youth and... he has had no opportunity of cultivating Letters." James Cook, *The Voyages of Captain James Cook*, Vol. I, William Smith, London, 1842.

Was the timing of Cook senior's move complete coincidence, or was there more? Certainly, he is part of a Scottish diaspora so evident in the eighteenth century.

Thirty years later in summer 1745, even as young James started as an apprentice, another Jacobite uprising was underway. It culminated in the battle at Culloden the next April, where the atrocities committed in the Highlands by a victorious English army are legend: the terrain all the way to Inverness was littered with mutilated bodies not only of Scots combatants, but farm workers, cottagers, young mothers, children, anyone in the vicinity. Then came calculated reprisals. A hundred and twenty Scots were hanged, over a thousand were transported for life, hundreds more rotted away in prison, four Scots peers—Lords Kilmarnock, Cromarty, Lovat, Balmerino—were hauled to London for show trials, while the officers of the rebel Manchester Regiment were hanged, drawn and quartered before a cockney mob, their heads impaled on pikes at Temple Bar (two of the bleached skulls overlooked the Strand for decades, only falling off in the late 1770s[93]). Across the north, rebels were pursued, their cots torched, their livestock stolen, their land seized. Wearing tartan and speaking Gaelic were made illegal, Highland chieftains were disempowered, clans fractured, forced clearances commenced. A whole way of life was stamped out as Britain formed mechanisms for colonial control.

Biographers make much of young James Cook's experiences as a shop assistant at Staithes; how it was in that fishing village his gift at mathematics emerged; how he met there and lined up a job with a prosperous coal-shipper—the decision that saw his nautical career begin.[94] Those biographers say nothing of

---

[93] Those two officers' skulls were the last heads to sit on Temple Bar before the practice halted in the late 18th century. (see Liza Picard, *Dr Johnson's London: Everyday Life in London 1740-1770*, Wiedenfeld & Nicholson, London, 2000, pp. 5-6.)

[94] The overarching biographers' agenda is set by J.C. Beaglehole's authoritative *The Life of Captain James Cook* (1974), most who have written on Cook in the fifty plus years since offering condensed versions of his account of the navigator's life before the navy. This is evident even in the most recent thorough biography, Frank McLynn's *Captain Cook: Master of the Seas* (Yale University Press, New Haven, 2011).

the Scottish question which dominated English politics and journalism over the same months, finding poignant outlet in the popular ballad 'The Tears of Scotland'.[95] This was a serious matter for the inhabitants of Staithes, because Scots refugees appeared in every harbour along that stretch of coast: Blyth, Tynemouth, Sunderland, Seaham, Hartlepool, Tees Bay, Whitby, so many more. Entire families were adrift, destitute and forlorn, some unable to understand English, seeking safety, harried by authority, driven to begging and petty crime. (The novelist Emily Bronte's fictional character Heathcliff, a swarthy urchin of unkempt 'gypsy aspect' found at a harbour side, who speaks a strange tongue and nurses an innate connectedness to wild moorlands, is a lingering echo of those refugee Scots.)

Was young James Cook, himself a child of the Scottish diaspora, in some way affected by these ethnic tensions? Those who met him throughout adulthood instantly registered his parentage: the lean taut frame, rich russet hair tied behind in a queue, the brune brows above piercing hazel eyes, those high Scots cheekbones. So did what was occurring across Northern coastal villages shape the apprentice who was about to switch retail trade for shipping? Did seeing those dispossessed, impoverished peoples at Staithes leave an impression on him? Like much about the navigator's career, we have the record of his actions yet we cannot read his thoughts, tapping the underlying motivations.

It is from James Cook the modern world gets the scientific expedition.[96] Each voyage saw him assemble a mixed team of

---

[95] Mourn, hapless Caledonia mourn/ Thy banished peace, thy laurels torn!/ Thy sons, for valour long renowned,/ Lie slaughtered on their native ground;/ Thy hospitable roofs no more/ Invite the stranger to the door;/ In smoky ruins sunk they lie,/ The monuments of cruelty.

[96] In discussing Cook's voyages we need to be conscious of how language has shifted over time. Where we now use the term 'science', in Cook's day the phrase 'natural philosophy' was employed instead. Likewise we find that 'Voyage of discovery', the expression then used to describe Cook's travels, referred not to discovering or finding new territory, but to making scientific discoveries in new lands. So our present day equivalent phrase is 'scientific expedition'.

specialists who were to take observations, collect samples and keep accurate records as they travelled through new lands. To support this he also ensured his ships were fitted out as mobile laboratories, being equipped with the most up-to-date apparatus to examine and measure, as well as safely storing those botanical, zoological and geological materials to be carried back to Britain for further analysis. This approach to research in the field was not only new, it was transformative: exploratory travel before his voyages, and exploratory travel after his voyages were just not the same. Indeed, by his third expedition it was apparent Cook had become—like Galileo—a human hinge on which scientific endeavour had pivoted.

Glory surrounds the 'experimental gentlemen' the navigator recruited for his expeditions, including Joseph Banks, Dr Daniel Solander, Dr Johann Forster and George Forster. Yet Cook always took aboard at least two astronomers, a scientific illustrator and a mathematician, each an ace in their discipline (data from observations taken in Tahiti enabled the earth's distance from the sun to be finally, and precisely, calculated). And there were skilled assistants whose task it was to collect samples, record, and process information. A capable astronomer himself, Cook expected his officers to have a secondary skill, either in astronomy, geology or natural history, to be used on the voyage. Even sailors or marines who picked up Polynesian phrases were expected to contribute to a growing lexicon of Pacific words (for which they were offered a place on the next voyage).

If our understanding of the natural world is indebted to Cook's restless work, public opinion of him as a person is sinking. This is evident nowadays among young people and those entering university. They get little history in school, and what they do pick up only fosters cultural self-loathing: 'White people must be demonised' seems an educational principle. Besides, young people assume their own era is highly sophisticated, and they will underrate the potential complexity of those who lived in past times.

It is different when you teach cultural history, students expecting imaginative and psychological depths to works of art studied, and related examples of literature or music. Yet when tackling certain historical periods, one can detect among undergraduates an unstated belief in our supposed moral superiority. —On such weeks I sometimes made mischief; like when we grappled with English art of the eighteenth century and I would set students unpicking William Hogarth's *Marriage á la Mode* or *Four Times of the Day*, analysing the pictures' Georgian wit. Some really delighted in Hogarth's urbane cleverness which struck them as advanced, almost present day. Toward that seminar's end I would introduce this passage on the Maoris of New Zealand, saying it was penned just a decade after Hogarth's death, inviting class discussion and asking for suggestions on its author:

> we debauch their Morals already too prone to vice and we interduce among them wants and perhaps diseases which they never before knew and which serves only to disturb that happy tranquillity they and their fore Fathers had injoy'd. If any one denies the truth of this assertion let him tell me what the Natives of the whole extent of America have gained by the commerce they have had with Europeans.[97]

That was written by James Cook. This was when he returned to Queen Charlotte Sound in June 1773, and he was musing over the natives he had befriended there, how in such a short time the process of trade was visibly corrupting them and their culture.[98]

---

[97] Beaglehole, *Journals of Cook*, vol. 2, p. 175. Written on the day after he sailed from New Zealand, Wednesday June 2, 1773, this complaint appears at the end of several pages reflecting on what Cook has observed of the Maoris since his previous visit to the same anchorage, aboard the *Endeavour*, four years earlier. Just prior to the quotation he expresses his distress over a visible increase in prostitution. Where on his previous stop over little prostitution had occurred between sailors and natives, and it seemed to be at the female Maori's discretion, it was now rife, and openly controlled by dominant male Maoris.

[98] Johann Forster himself was later moved to write that, given how contact was adversely affecting native cultures, it might be 'better for the discoverers, and the discovered, that the South Seas had still remained unknown to Europe and its restless inhabitants'. Forster, J.G.A., *A Voyage Round the World*, London, 1777, vol. 1, p. 368; Joppien & Smith, *Art of Cook's Voyages*, vol. 2, p. 40.

It shocked him, shocked him deeply. Indeed, far from supporting European colonisation, Cook points to the whole of America and declares that for natives nothing good has come of it.

The passage always surprised my students. In its emphatic concern it challenged certainties they held not only about Europeans of the period, but James Cook. A sensitivity was revealed here that struck students as so modern, and morally enlightened. The individual revealed in that passage doesn't match perceptions now circulating. Believing one must seek to understand other peoples in the light of their circumstances, Cook did not pass judgement on native cultures.[99] As a proto-scientist himself he sought to understand. Just because Maoris or Tahitians had lifestyles different to Europeans, didn't for him amount to their being inferior. We find this increasingly voiced in his journals. In fact, the more time he spent with natives, the more convinced Cook was of this outlook. From their subsequent writings, its apparent Cook was talking over the matter with the Forsters, Anders Sparrman and William Wales on the second voyage.

Decades ago the Marxist historian Bernard Smith pointed to how criticism of Cook has repeatedly come from persons who vilify him in order to advance their own agendas.[100] Some make him a scapegoat for things he took no part in: witness how social justice warriors now blame Cook for European colonisation of the Pacific, although this would be like convicting Albert Einstein for nuclear weapons. We surely need to distinguish between the pioneering navigator—who was *not* an advocate of colonisation—and the culture that came after his death. Besides, in studying his scientific expeditions we sometimes find Europeans did not always begin what they are accused of.

Take environmental degradation. Easter Island was a sorry place when Cook's *Resolution* dropped anchor there in 1774.

---
[99] Porter, *Enlightenment*, p. 362.
[100] Smith, *Imagining the Pacific*, p. 239.

Natives had deforested the land over generations, so it no longer supported the lush jungle common on islands at that latitude. This loss of habitat, combined with native hunting, had seen the passing of animal species unique to the island. Actually, prehistoric migration caused many extinctions across the Pacific, as discussed even by the revered Jared Diamond in his best-selling *Guns, Germs and Steel* (1997). There used to be flightless birds throughout Polynesia, including the moa of New Zealand and the land geese of Hawaii. Native occupation saw them hunted out, while large seal populations also dwindled on settled islands.[101] The most widescale zoological extinctions occurred in Australia where the arrival of humans from Asia sounded a death knell, especially for resident megafauna.[102]

The vanishing of native utopias, which are said to have existed before Cook's expeditions, is more slippery. In his watershed book *Orientalism* (1978), the intellectual foundation for identity politics, Edward Said pointed out how the Pacific has long acted as a screen on which the West projects its cultural fantasies. So the scientific expeditions of Louis de Bougainville and James Cook were conducted against an immense corpus of 'travel literature, imaginary utopias, moral voyages ... [and] innumerable speculations on giants, Patagonians, savages, natives and monsters.'[103] Those popular myths wouldn't go away, as was evident when John Hawkesworth falsified recent information from Pacific exploration to reaffirm tales of idyllic societies and bizarre peoples in the South Seas. Mind you, Cook himself wasn't above massaging material; as seen he had the artist on the *Resolution* contrive paintings to give an idealised view of tribal life in the Pacific. So the puzzle should not be what happened to those

---

[101] Jared Diamond, *Guns, Germs and Steel: A Short History of Everybody for the Last 13,000 Years*, Chatto & Windus, London, 1997, pp. 59-60.

[102] Ibid., pp. 44, 110. 304, 308. It is common to point an accusing finger at early British colonists for exterminating the Tasmanian Tiger, although Aboriginals had long before hunted out the animal on Australia's mainland.

[103] Edward Said, *Orientalism*, Routledge & Kegan Paul, London, 1978, p. 117.

utopias, but whether—as Edward Said and the postmodernists hold—they were and continue to be imaginative projections. Like Paul Gauguin's painted visions of Polynesians dwelling in spiritual rhythm with a shimmering, wildly coloured landscape, current stories of lost native paradises represent the escapist dream of urbanised and increasingly high-tech Westerners.[104]

What one also repeatedly notices when closely studying those expeditions is how James Cook made such an effort to establish cordial relations with Pacific peoples. Political activists today insinuate he and his crew ran amok in foreign parts like the hyper-masculine, hard-drinking Americans of current action movies. However, the journals of naval officers and other travellers on Cook's expeditions show he took a dim view of swagger or aggression. Tars who stepped out of line were flogged, and midshipmen sent before-the-mast (that is, demoted). As for contact with natives, the navigator strove to assure them he came in peace; and when hostilities did occur, there followed efforts to effect a quick and constructive reconciliation. Grudges toward natives were not tolerated, crewmen being told to set aside grievances.

Cook's visit to New Zealand on his third expedition deserves especial study, particularly how he acted toward chief Kahura. When they met the navigator was dignified and respectful to the native. Cook quietly listened as the warrior volunteered his account of what happened with Rowe's shore party and admitted to cannibalism. Then, far from seeking revenge, and punishing this ring-leader for massacring and eating ten sailors, Cook publicly forgave the Maori. Putting violence behind them, Cook next honoured Kahura by directing John Webber to make the Maori's portrait, thereby sealing a peaceful reconciliation with this feared

---

[104] The British cultural historian Peter Ackroyd has recently pointed out that the urban middle-class psyche of the twentieth century became fixated with a nostalgia for largely imaginary versions of traditional rural life. Indeed, this has increased the more rural cultures were destroyed. Peter Ackroyd, *The History of England: Vol. VI, Innovation*, Pan Macmillan, London, 2022, pp. 15-16.

warrior. The navigator and the native had parted amicably when the *Resolution* set sail the next day.[105]

With that remarkable meeting, and his public act of forgiveness, might we therefore say James Cook started the historical process of reconciliation? Certainly as a practical instance of reconciliation-in-action Cook offers here a valuable model for positive behaviour upon indigenous issues. The peoples of Australia and New Zealand would do well to reflect upon it.

---

[105] Kahura and his extended family were according to Beaglehole the last visitors aboard ship, the chief disembarking just before Cook's departure. Beaglehole, *Journals of Cook*, vol. 4, p. 524.

Crew members disciplined by Cook for abuses against natives.

HMS Endeavour 1768-72

April 29, 1769.	Henry Jeffs, ship's butcher: a dozen lashes for assaulting a Tahitian woman.[106]
June 12, 1769.	James Nicholson, seaman; John Thurman [or Thurmond], seaman: two dozen lashes each for stealing items from Tahitians, including plaited hair, bows and arrows.
November 30, 1769.	Matthew Cox, seaman; Manoel Pereira [or Paroya], seaman; Henry Stephens, seaman: a dozen lashes each for digging up and stealing potatoes from a Maori plantation in the Bay of Islands.

* * * * *

HMS Resolution 1772-75

November 22, 1773.	Richard Lee, seaman: a dozen lashes for theft from a Maori of a hatchet and other traded articles.
August 18, 1774.	William Tow, Marine: a dozen lashes for illegal trades with natives in the New Hebrides.
August 19, 1774.	William Wedgeborough, Marine: two months in irons for the unauthorised shooting of a native youth at Tana.[107]

---

[106] The Tahitian woman was shocked by the violence she had to watch, pleading for leniency against her attacker.

[107] Wedgeborough was hit in the arm by an arrow while standing guard. He instantly reacted, shooting dead the first native he saw. But the man was innocent of the attack, so Cook was furious.

HMS Resolution 1776-79

June 23, 1777.	John Brown, Quartermaster: a dozen lashes for striking a Tongan chief.
September 12, 1777.	William Doyle, Boatswain's mate: a dozen lashes for causing disturbances among Tahitians and neglect of duty.
September 29, 1777.	William Doyle, Boatswain's mate: six lashes for striking a Tahitian chief.
January 5, 1779.	James Dermot, seaman: a dozen lashes for cheating Hawaiians in trade.
January 25, 1779.	William Bradley, seaman: two dozen lashes for having sex with Hawaiian women after being forbidden to do so because he had a venereal infection.

Cook made naval punishment into a public display in the South Seas. Offending crew were flogged not only before the ship's company, but natives who had been wronged, their family members and local chiefs were also present.

Paper Trails

On matters of evidence

Doubt now hangs over Lieutenant James Burney. Some historians have reassessed his actions when searching for the crewmen missing in Queen Charlotte Sound. The twenty-three-year-old naval officer is said to have lead a massacre of Maoris before even finding human remains. This is how the biographer Frank McLynn describes the incident in his 2011 book *Captain Cook: Master of the Seas*:

> just before dusk they came on around 200 Maoris gathered as if for a festivity. When they taunted the approaching boat party, Burney gave the order to open fire. Muskets, musketoons and wall-guns scythed through the packed ranks of Maoris, causing the survivors to run for cover in the trees. Once the beach was clear Burney reconnoitred and found the eyes, hearts, lungs, livers and entrails of their comrades roasting on fires. Reeling from the horror and fearing a counter-attack they re-embarked on the launch, first destroying the dozens of canoes drawn up on the beach ...[108]

Firing upon natives who were only taunting the Europeans was inhumane. Worse still, the weapons employed were barbarous. You did not turn a musketoon on people. A forerunner of the shotgun, it was for hunting birds and small prey. Cook's crew used a musketoon to disable native canoes when needed, firing a spray of pellets to puncture the hull and cause it to sink. Then there was the smooth bore wall-gun. A single shot by a wall-gun could cut a man in two at a hundred yards—which is why it was not turned on people. This heavy calibre firearm with quite a range was used for protection against potentially aggressive larger animals, like elephant seals and walruses. Officers on Cook's voyages sometimes used a wall-gun as a percussive signal. A weapon loaded only with powder would be discharged into the air to hail any crew ashore who ventured out of sight. The booming noise carried far.

McLynn lists among his few sources for this episode Anne Salmond's history *The Trial of the Cannibal Dog: Captain Cook*

---

[108] McLynn, *Master of the Seas*, pp. 224-5.

in the South Seas (2003). That book supplies further detail. When recounting Burney's search for the missing men, Professor Salmond portrays a naval officer who fires on natives without provocation:

> By now it was almost dusk. They rowed the launch to Grass Cove, the adjacent bay, where they found canoes hauled up on the beach and hundreds of people gathered along the shore and on the hillside ... As the launch approached the beach some people began to taunt the sailors, calling out and gesturing for them to come ashore. Burney ordered his men to fire muskets and musketoons at will into the crowd. At the first volley the people seemed stunned; at the second volley they broke and ran for the trees, howling with fear and pain. The wall-guns were then loaded and fired, and the marines kept on shooting until nobody was left in sight. Burney left Fannin, the ship's master, to guard the boat, and searched the beach with a party of marines. They found one of the cutter's oars broken and stuck upright in the ground... Dogs were chewing the discarded entrails of four or five men, and they found the eyes, hearts, lungs, livers and heads of their comrades, including the head of Furneaux's black servant, various feet, and Rowe's left hand (identified by its scarred forefinger) roasting on fires or scattered on the ground. Fannin called out that he could hear people shouting in the valley, perhaps preparing to attack, so they hastily gathered up some of these body parts and hurried back to the launch. They fired one last volley at a large crowd of people gathered on a hillside up the valley, and left the cove in darkness...[109]

Salmond's description suggests the massacre was even worse than McLynn portrayed. She writes that the marines from the *Adventure* used muskets <u>and</u> musketoons when firing two volleys directly into a crowd numbering hundreds of natives.[110] The marines then changed to wall-guns to clear the shore of Maoris,

---

[109] Salmond, *Trial of the Cannibal Dog*, p. 229.
[110] On the number of Maoris, in her previous book Salmond wrote that when Burney's search party rowed into Grassy Cove 'a crowd of hundreds (or according to Furneaux, fifteen hundred to two thousand) were gathered on the hillside'. Anne Salmond, *Between Worlds: Early Exchanges between Maori and Europeans 1773-1815*, Viking, New Zealand, 1997, p. 103.

shooting without break 'until nobody was left in sight.'[111] Later, after making their gruesome discovery on the beach, the marines fired a further volley at the remaining natives who now were gathered on an adjacent hill.

Where did the information used by McLynn and Salmond come from? Comparing their texts with historical records from the *Adventure*, journals differ significantly from them on that afternoon's search. This is—in its entirety—what Commander Furneaux wrote after Burney's party returned to the ship:

> Hoisted out the Launch & sent her with the 2ᵈ Lieuᵗ mann'd with the Boats Crew and Ten Marines in search of her [the missing boat], who returned about 7 o'clock the same night with the melancholy news of her being cut off by the Indians in Grass Cove whence they found the Relicks of several and the intrails of five men lying on the beach and in Canoes they found several baskets of human flesh and five odd shoes new, as our people had been served Shoes a day or two before; they brought on board several hands, two of which we knew, one belonged to Thomas Hill being marked on the Back T.H. another to Mʳ Rowe who had a wound on his fore finger not quite whole, and the Head, which was supposed to be the head of my servant by the high forhead he being a Negroe, the Launch fired on them where they were assembled in great numbers on the top of a hill making all signs of joy imaginable. Next morning unmoored and weighed ...[112]

William Bayly, the astronomer on the *Adventure*, also entered in his journal a summary of what Burney and others in his party told the denizens of the quarterdeck.

> [December] 18ᵗʰ in the morning the Long-boat was sent well manned & armed in search of her [the missing boat]. The first cove they went into there was 3 canoes laying on the beach. The Indians behaved friendly at first but rather saucy at our boats

---

[111] Salmond confuses the long range wall-gun with a swivel gun, an anti-personnel weapon mounted in a bracket on the ship and used to repel close quarters attacks. Salmond, *Trial of the Cannibal Dog*, p. 2.
[112] Beaglehole, *Journals of Cook*, vol. 2, app. IV, pp. 743-4.

departure, but the officer took no notice of it. The next bay they entered were 7 or 8 canoes on the beach & many Indians who behaved very sivil. Going out of this cove our people obs'd a large canoe coming toward them but when the Indians saw them they ran the canoe into a little creek & fled to the Woods and disappeared, which made our people suspect something was the occasion. On inspecting into the contents of the Canoe they found baskets full of roasted human flesh & in one of them was a mans hand cut off a little above the rist on the Back of which was T.H. in Roman letters, which was directly known to be one of the boats crew's hand viz. Thomas Hill's. This discovery convinced our people that the boats crew was destroyed. They broke the canoe to pieces & proceeded to Grass Cove (from whence the canoe seemed to come), where was a great many number of Indians to the amount of an hundred or more, making merry, dancing & skipping about on a little hill near the beach. As soon as our boat came near the shore they invited them to shore but our people fired a broadside at them & a second which they seemed not to mind notwithstanding several fell down. They then fired two wall pieces loaded with a number of pistol balls & the Marines kept up a brisk fire which put them to flight, they making a great cry. They saw several crawling on their hands and knees into the Bushes & the dead was dragged off. Our people went on shore & found the Intrails of 4 or 5 men together with the Hearts & Lungs & 3 heads roasted, one of which appeared to be the Capt's Black servant by its make. They found the left hand of a man which was known to be Mr. Rowe's by a cut out of the middle of the fore finger which was just healed up. They likewise found some feet & other parts but all much defaced by roasting except one foot. They demolished the canoes there & night coming on they returned on board with the melancholy news.[113]

Lieutenant Burney's journal, the only written account by someone at the scene, has a detailed entry on the day's search. It runs to several pages in the second volume of J.C. Beaglehole's *The Journals of Captain Cook*. After relating his party's fruitless efforts to locate the missing crewmen through morning then the

---

[113] Robert McNabb ed., *Historical Records of New Zealand*, vol. 2, pp. 217-8.

afternoon, checking a succession of coves along Queen Charlotte Sound, Burney shifts tone when they spot a canoe as sunset approaches:

> we went ashore & Searchd the Canoe where we found one of the Rullock ports of the Cutter & some Shoes one of which was known to belong to Mr Woodhouse, one of our Midshipmen, who went with Mr Rowe—one of the people at the same time brought me a piece of meat, which he took to be some of the Salt Meat belonging to the Cutter's Crew—on examining this and smelling to it I found it was fresh meat—Mr Fannin (the Master) who was with me, supos'd it was Dog's flesh & I was of the same opinion, for I still doubted their being Cannibals: but we were Soon convinced by most horrid & undeniable proofs—a great many baskets (about 20) laying on the beach tied up, we cut them open, some were full of roasted flesh & some of fern root which serves them for bread—on further search we found more shoes & a hand which we immediately knew to have belong'd to Thos Hill one of our Forecastlemen, it being marked T.H. which he had got done at Otaheite with a tattow instrument—I went with some of the people a little way up to the woods, but saw nothing else... [114]

Finding nothing more, and fearful for their safety, Burney and his men returned to the launch then began rowing back to the *Adventure*. Within minutes things would change:

> On opening the next bay, which was Grass Cove, we saw 4 Canoes—one Single & 3 double ones—a great many People on the beach—a large fire was on top of the High Land beyond the woods, from whence all the way down the Hill the place thronged like a Fair—as we came in, I order'd a Musketoon to be fired through one of the Canoes, as we suspected they might be full of men laying down in the bottom, but nobody was seen in them—the Savages on the little hill still kept hollowing and making Signs for us to come ashore—however as soon as we got close in we all fired—the first Volley did not seem to affect them much—but on the 2^d they began to scramble away as fast

---

[114] Beaglehole, *Journals of Cook*, vol. 2, app. IV, p. 750.

as they could, some of them howling—we continued firing as long as we could see the least glimpse of a man through the bushes—amongst the Indians were 2 very stout men who never offer'd to move till they found themselves forsaken by their companions & and then they walkd away with great composure and deliberation—their pride not Suffering them to run…[115]

The boat landed then Burney took eight of the marines ashore to reconnoitre:

> on the beach were 2 bundles of Cellery which had been gather'd for the loading the Cutter—a plain proof that the attack was made here—a broken piece of an Oar was stuck upright in the Ground to which they had tied their Canoes—I then searchd all along the back of the beach to see if the Cutter was there—we found no boat—but instead of her—Such a shocking scene of Carnage & Barbarity as can never be mentiond or thought of, but with horror.[116]

> at leaving Grass Cove we had fired a general Volley towards where we had heard the Indians talking—but by going in & out of the boat the Arms had got wet and some 4 of the pieces mist fire—what was still worst it began to rain…[117]

The difference between these accounts, especially Burney's, and the episode as portrayed by Salmond and McLynn, is serious. Facts are different—critical facts on which the historians rely. Salmond and McLynn have the entire incident play out on a single beach, although Burney and Bayly describe successive events in two different bays. Burney does not indicate the number of Maoris; or have marines use musketoons and wall-guns against the natives. Bayly writes there were 'an hundred or more' natives; and wall guns were fired at distant natives, although they were loaded to spray small gauge balls (not shoot the lethal large calibre bullet). Where Salmond and McLynn describe a massacre, Burney and Bayly remark that the Maoris

---

[115] Beaglehole, *Journals of Cook*, vol. 2, app. IV, p. 751.
[116] Ibid.
[117] Ibid., p.752.

were not much affected when volleys were fired at them, some making a show of casually strolling out of range.

We have grounds to believe the young officer here: chief Kahura said much the same when he met with James Cook four years later in February 1777. By Kahura's own account no massacre of Maoris occurred, the chief boasting that none of the gathered warriors were injured when Burney's party shot at them. As corroborating proof goes you cannot get stronger.

Where did Salmond and McLynn obtain information? If material from Burney's journal is in the mix, they also use particulars from an anonymous article published in London upon the *Adventure*'s return. Appearing in December 1774's edition of *The Monthly Miscellany*, it was headed: 'AUTHENTIC ACCOUNT OF THE FATE OF TEN MEN, belonging to the ADVENTURE, lately returned from the SOUTH SEAS, who were Eaten by the SAVAGES in NEW ZEALAND,' followed by the explanation 'Extracted from the JOURNAL of one of the CREW, that was ordered to make Search for the UNHAPPY SUFFERERS.' This is the account it gives of Burney's search party in Queen Charlotte Sound:

> At day break, the captain ordered the long boat to be hoisted out, and double manned, with Mr Burney, Second Lieutenant, Mr Freeman, master, the corporal of marines, with five private men, all well armed, with plenty of ammunition, two wall pieces, and three days provision.
>
> Thus equipped, about nine in the morning we left the ship, and sailed and towed [rowed] for East-Bay, keeping close in shore, and examining every creek we passed, to find the cutter. We continued our search until two in the afternoon, when we put into a small cove to dress dinner. While that was getting ready, we observed a company of Indians, seemingly very busy, on the opposite shore; we left our dinner and rowed precipitately to the place where the savages were assembled. On our approach they all fled; we followed them closely to a little town which we found deserted; we searched their huts, and while thus

employed the savages returned, and made a shew of resistence; but some trifling presents being made to their chiefs they were very soon appeased. However, on our return to our boat, they followed us, and some of them threw stones. After we had dined, we renewed our search, and at proper intervals fired our wall-pieces, as signals to the cutter, if any of her people should happen to be within hearing.

About five in the afternoon we opened a small bay, whence we saw a large double canoe, and a body of Indians hauling her upon the beach. We quickened our course to come up with them, but the savages instantly fled on seeing us approach: this made us suspect some mischief had been done. On landing, the first thing we saw in the canoe, was one of the cutters rowlock-boards, and a pair of shoes tied up together. On advancing farther up the beach, we found several of their baskets, and saw one of their dogs eating a piece of broiled flesh. We examined it, and suspected it to be human; and in one of their baskets, having found a hand, which we knew to be the left hand of Thomas Hill, by the letters T. H. being marked on it, we were no longer in doubt about the event. We pursued the savages as far as was practicable; but without success. On our return we destroyed their canoe, and continued our search.

At half after six in the evening we opened Grass-cove, where we saw a great many Indians assembled on the Beach, and six or seven canoes floating in the surf. We stood in shore, and as soon as the savages saw us, they retreated to a rising hill, close by the water-side. We were in doubt, whether it was in fear they retreated, or with a design to decoy us to an ambuscade. Our Lieutenant being determined not to be surprized, and therefore, running close to the shore, ordered the grappling to be dropt near enough to reach them with our guns, but at too great a distance to be under any apprehensions from their treachery. In this position we began to engage, taking aim, and determining to kill as many of them as our guns could reach. It was sometime before we dislodged them; but at length many of them being wounded, and some killed, they began to disperse. Our Lieutenant improved their panic, and, supported by the officers and marines, leapt on shore, and pursued the fugitives.

We had not advanced far from the water side, before we beheld the most horrid sight that ever was seen by any European; the heads, hearts, livers and lights [eyes] of three or four of our people broiling on the fire, and their bowels lying at a distance of about six yards from the fire, with several of their hands and limbs in a mangled condition, some broiled, some raw; but no other parts of their bodies, which gave cause to suspect that the cannibals had feasted on and eaten all the rest.

We observed a large body of them assembled on the top of a hill, at about two miles distance; but night coming on, we durst not advance to attack them; neither was it thought safe to quit the shore, to take account of the number killed, our body being but small, and the savages numerous and fierce. They were armed with long lances, and with weapons not unlike the halberts of our serjeants in shape, made of hard wood, and instead of iron, mounted with bone. We could discover nothing belonging to the cutter, but one of the oars, which was broken and stuck in the sand, and fastenings of the Indians canoes tied to it.

It was suspected that the dead bodies of our people had been divided among the different parties of savages that had been concerned in the massacre; and it was not improbable but that the party that was seen at a distance were feasting upon some of the others, as those on shore had been upon what were found, before they were disturbed by our crew of the long-boat. Be that as it may, we could discover no traces of more than four of their bodies, nor could we tell where the savages concealed the cutter.

It was now near night, and our lieutenant not thinking it safe to trust the crew in the dark, in a open boat, within reach of such cruel barbarians, ordered the canoes to be broken up and destroyed; and after carefully collecting the remains of our mangled companions, we made best of our way from this polluted place. About four the next morning we weighed anchor, and about seven got underway, and pursued our course home. In the mean time, the surgeons examined the remains of the bodies brought on board, but could not make out to whom they belonged; so they were decently laid together, and with the usual solemnity on board ships, commited to the deep.[118]

This unattributed account was reused within an anonymous narrative of the full voyage rushed into print after the return of Cook's *Resolution* in August 1775.[119] Its London publisher issued the book under the title *Journal of the* Resolution's *Voyage in 1772, 1773, 1774 and 1775, & Journal of the* Adventure's *Voyage in 1772, 1773, and 1774, on Discovery to the Southern Hemisphere*.[120] Good sales saw the book re-published in Dublin the next year, followed by a French translation appearing in Amsterdam during 1776.

Cook and his superiors at the Admiralty were perturbed by this illicit, at points inaccurate text. Naval crew were not to publish their own accounts of a voyage without permission, in fact, any journals, maps or drawings they made were surrendered to the Admiralty at journey's end to prevent publication and keep military information secure. The Admiralty was particularly concerned about the sensationalist description of finding the remains of Rowe's party, which included graphic details Lieutenant Burney withheld from his own written report. These particulars alarmed and distressed the British public.

The ships' officers read the entire book, trying to identify its author. To them the narrative was a patchwork. Some of the text was accurate, some distorted through retelling, some just sailors' gossip. Certain incidents had evidently been witnessed, although there was much rhetorical padding. Persons from both vessels had contributed sections, navigational details on their paths being set with chunks of narrative on how each fared. The question was which crew members composed this unauthorised text?

---

[118] *Monthly Miscellany*, Dec. 1774, pp. 297-8.
[119] There are minor editorial changes, including an adjustment in grammar, 'we' and 'our' in the journal article becoming 'they' in the book.
[120] Anon. (John Marra), *Journal of the* Resolution's *Voyage in 1772, 1773, 1774 and 1775, & Journal of the* Adventure's *Voyage in 1772, 1773, and 1774, on Discovery to the Southern Hemisphere* (London, 1775), reprinted Da Capo Press, New York, 1967, pp. 92-6.

James Cook's suspicions were raised by the slant taken on a number of incidents, and a passing favourable remark made about one sailor, John Marra. They led him to believe Marra had a hand in writing the book. This Able Seaman in his early twenties, who served as Gunner's mate on the *Resolution*, had previously been described by Cook as 'An Irishman by birth, a good seaman and had Saild both in the English and Dutch Service.'[121] But rum could stir Marra to recklessness. He tried to jump ship at Deptford before the two vessels had even sailed to Portsmouth for final fitting out. Over the subsequent voyage, in addition to warnings for minor misbehaviour, Marra received a dozen lashes for insolence off Madeira (3 Aug. 1772), another six lashes for the same in Tahiti (30 Aug. 1773), spent a fortnight in irons for desertion when drunk on a repeat visit to Tahiti (12 May 1774), and, months later, received a dozen more lashes for drunkenly going ashore at Queen Charlotte Sound without permission (3 Nov. 1774). Cook was thoroughly fed up with the man when the last incident occurred. One midshipman, John Elliott, wrote of overhearing the Captain say of Marra 'if he was not well assurd that the fellow would be killd and Eat, before Morning, he would have let him go.'[122]

Marra had not been present at assorted events described in the book. For our purposes, as a crewman aboard Cook's *Resolution* he was not on the same vessel as Lieutenant Burney, and so could not have known of the troubles in New Zealand until his ship picked up garbled news from a Dutch merchant in the Indian Ocean. Nevertheless, as the sole identified co-author, Marra's name has been attached to the unauthorised book ever since.

Many modern historians use the Marra text quite freely when recounting the search for Rowe's party. Few have qualms about its authorship and reliability. In this vein, if Anne Salmond and Frank McLynn use Burney's journal, the Marra text is the main source for their accounts of conflict between natives and

---

[121] Beaglehole, *Journals of Cook,* vol. 2, p. 876.
[122] Beaglehole, *Journals of Cook,* vol 4, p. 422.

the search party. They also rely entirely on its description of finding the sailors' butchered bodies, Professor Salmond being taken with two very short graphic passages. In the first, Burney 'saw one of the dogs eating a piece of broiled flesh, which upon examining they suspected to be human'; and in the second, the searchers 'beheld the most horrible sight that ever was seen by any European; the heads, hearts, livers and lights [eyes] of three or four of their people broiling on the fire, and their bowels lying at a distance of about six yards from the fire, with several of their hands and limbs...'[123] (On the matter of authorship, readers will notice similarities between the Marra text here and the account quoted in Bayly's journal which suggests a common voice.)

Far from repeating either passage when describing the incident, Salmond embellishes. Where the original description reproduced in the second volume of Beaglehole's *The Journals of Captain Cook* had a single dog eating one piece of broiled flesh, Salmond's study *Between Worlds: Early Exchanges between Maori and Europeans* (1997) sees this become 'dogs [were] chewing on the roasted hearts, lungs, heads, hands and feet of their comrades'; while her next book *The Trial of the Cannibal Dog: Captain Cook in the South Seas* (2003) saw this worked into 'Dogs were chewing at the discarded entrails of four or five men, and they found the eyes, hearts, lungs, livers and heads of their comrades...'[124] The second mention is accompanied by a period illustration, with the caption: 'The *Adventure*'s men find the remains of their comrades at Grass Cove.'[125] It shows ten Europeans with muskets standing together to the right, a sailing ship at anchor in centre distance, and on the left, midway back and unseen by the men, a pale dog chewing at a shapeless blob. That image reproduced and used by Salmond had been borrowed from the original 1775 Marra book.

---

[123] Marra, *Journal of the* Resolution's *Voyage*, pp. 94–5.
[124] Salmond, *Between Worlds*, p. 103; Salmond, *Trial of the Cannibal Dog*, p. 229.
[125] Salmond, *Trial of the Cannibal Dog*, p. 230. In the Marra book, the illustration appeared on a single-sided sheet between pages 94 and 95.

Despite the use Salmond makes of the Marra text, she does know it to be unreliable. Salmond tells the reader this—twice. Among her endnotes at the back of *Between Worlds* is this qualifying sentence on the purported massacre: 'It does not seem likely that Marra was in fact an eyewitness, however, so there was some creative editing.'[126] Likewise in her book *The Trial of the Cannibal Dog*, an endnote on the same incident runs: 'Marra was not an eyewitness, however, although he was drawing from an eyewitness account, and there may have been some creative editing.'[127] Given Salmond knows this, why does she rely on the Marra text?

The Marra book is hardly an isolated example of a blended text. Hearsay, invention and superstition loom large in early first hand accounts of Pacific voyages, although most fabrications are known. The more fanciful reports could be called out soon after publication. Take an attention-catching anonymous account of the just completed voyage of the *Dolphin*, the first European vessel to encounter Tahiti. It mentions seeing giants in Patagonia. Reputedly penned by a naval officer aboard, we now know one of the authors to be a teenage midshipman, the youthful Charles Clerke. And giants were slipped in as a prank.

Even apparently eyewitness accounts by identified authors could be unreliable. Upon reading the book just published by David Samwell, who replaced Dr Anderson as surgeon aboard the *Discovery*, a midshipman on the same voyage was indignant: 'Some things are represented … in situations which should seem to render minute detail impossible,' James Trevenen protested.[128] Alexander Home, a midshipman on the same vessel, was candid about liberties sometimes taken when writing his journal. In fact,

---

[126] Salmond, *Between Worlds*, p. 538.
[127] Salmond, *Trial of a Cannibal Dog*, p. 472.
[128] J.C. Beaglehole, *The Death of Captain James Cook*, Turnbull Library, Wellington, 1979, p. 17. Samwell, former surgeon's mate, was promoted to surgeon when Dr Anderson died of tuberculosis.

he attached this covering note to a detailed description of Cook's death:

> I was not present in this Fray being Sick So this Account is Entirely from the Mouths of others Who were present. But these Differed greatly in their Relation of the Same Matters So that what I have here said I do not Aver to be the Real truth in Every particul although in General it may be pretty Nigh the Matter. I have carefully Asserted such Relations as had the greatest appearance of Truth. But indeed they were Exceedingly perplexed in their Accounts that it was a hard Matter to Colect Certainty, in particular cases or indeed to write any Acc ount at all.[129]

Where certain information can be embellished or doubtful, some aspects of sea travel will be persistently missing from sailors' journals—especially information on other crew members. Some figures who served under James Cook went on to distinguished careers, so there is much material about them. But most midshipmen and sailors endure only as names in naval records. The appearance of a crewman, his height, build, gait, and complexion, as well as how he spoke, his temperament, any mannerisms—such things went unrecorded.[130] We are therefore fortunate that after the second voyage John Elliot, a teenage midshipman on the *Resolution* mentioned above, wrote out for his family a list of nearly every officer and gentleman accommodated in Cook's quarterdeck, with notes on their character; for example,

> Charles Clerke, 2nd Lieutenant, 25 yrs, A brave and good officer, & a genal favorite
>
> Richard Pickersgill, 3rd Lieutenant, 22 yrs, A good officer and astronomer, but liking ye Grog
>
> Mr Forster, Botanist, 45 yrs, A clever but a litigious quarelsom fellow

---

[129] Beaglehole, *Death of Cook*, p. 26.

[130] Formal portraits were later painted of several of the officers when they had risen in their careers and achieved a certain social standing, but often the outcome a typical execise in flattery, conveying little about the sitter's character and mannerisms.

John Whitehouse, Master's mate, 28 yrs, Jesuitical, sensible but an insinuating litigious mischief making fellow

Mr Maxwill, Midshipman, 17 yrs, An hypocrytical canting fellow

Charles Price, Midshipman, 15 yrs, Unsteady & drinking

Mr Vancouver, Midshipman, 13½ yrs, A Quiet inoffensive Young man

This confidential aside is highly valued. It reveals something of the personalities behind assorted names. Without it we would have nothing whatever on some of these individuals.

Junior officers and midshipmen were cautious about what they recorded in journals. The Captain of a vessel might keep an eye on those journals, checks being mandatory if a midshipman was monitored for promotion. And at the end of a voyage journals were returned to the Admiralty where they could be read by officials wanting to cross check incidents which affected the ship. If considered significant, passages from the journals of officers who lost their lives on a voyage were sometimes quoted in accounts published afterward. So those issued with journals refrained from making entries that might reflect poorly on themselves.

Daily entries in officers' journals mostly give a ship's position at midday, the weather, the distance travelled in the past twenty-four hours, and no more. What was happening between people on the vessel doesn't rate a mention. Popularist histories customarily portray working relations among the crew, showing some individuals as friends, even referring to supposed conversations they shared. Scouring journals no one aboard ship troubled to write down what crew members were like as individuals, let alone what they said to each other in those interminable weeks at sea. Friendships are a blank in most officers' journals, which is frustrating given how significant relationships often grew between persons serving together.

Lack of information doesn't stop there. Despite the efforts of many officers to note their observations when visiting islands, we don't have a single account in any of those documents, not one, of conversation around the captain's table over a meal. What Cook, his officers and the naturalists talked about when together is unrecorded. Discretion is the rule. This extends to all comments about the captain. When, during the final voyage, Cook's state of health began to deteriorate, and he intermittently acted out of character, little appears in crewmen's' journals. That his officers and the older sea hands had been anxious for his wellbeing we know from statements they made upon their return to Britain.

Most disconcerting for modern readers perusing officers' journals is how any reference to sailors' inner lives, to what they thought and felt as individuals, isn't related in the writings of those who travelled through the South Seas. A number of historians have referred to the feelings of officers and crew when they revisited Queen Charlotte Sound on the third voyage, that site for the massacre of Rowe's group: 'Many of the sailors, too, were thirsty for revenge,' Anne Salmond writes. 'They were outraged that people who had cooked and eaten their comrades should walk about unscathed.'[131] She may be correct, but she is jumping to conclusions; because no one at the time noted the feelings of the crew, either on the quarter deck, or among other ranks. Not even James Burney wrote his feelings at being back where the *Adventure*'s men had been massacred and eaten. He fills several pages with notes when there, but this writing is mostly about what the Maoris did during the day, and how they conducted themselves. Burney does not reveal his own feelings. Actually, apart from Joseph Banks on occasion, no one on any of Cook's voyages uses pen and paper to confide their thoughts. Introspection is missing.

There are reasons for these omissions—telling reasons which underline how ours is a different age. Of course, the late eighteenth century saw private experience increasingly valued across English

---

[131] Salmond, *Trial of the Cannibal Dog*, p. 3.

writing, from *belles lettres* through to prose fiction.[132] Longstanding strictures against intimacy were relaxed. People tried to write authentically, and revealingly, of their personal relationships and mental lives. However, men like Cook, Clerke and Burney were incapable of writing in the intimate, candid manner soon to be developed by Wordsworth, Coleridge and their followers. It was later generations of mariners who might confide such thoughts to journals, gradually embracing that introspection introduced by the Romantics.

Still, in their focus on naval activities, sailors' journals do bring to the fore routines of travel so often skipped over by modern authors. It is common for history writers to fix on what occurred between Cook's crew and natives during longer island stops; but they do not explain the immense toil necessitated by these breaks to sailing. Ship's repairs and foraging may get a cursory mention, and that is all. It takes a scholar with an eye on ship's journals, like Geoffrey Blainey, to point out the intensive work to be performed at these landings, and how this shaped the ongoing voyage:

> the *Endeavour* had been overhauled while anchored in Tahiti. During the repairs, all provisions and most of the other stores had been carried on to dry land, and now they were brought back and re-stowed. A ship on a long voyage was like a big warehouse, and as the warehouse went on and the warehouse became emptier, the use of space could be replanned. Now an area of the ship's deck was almost jammed with pigs, hens and other live stock bought in Tahiti.[133]

These stops for periodic maintenance and reorganisation were crucial. It is why on his second and third voyages Cook scheduled visits to Queen Charlotte Sound. He would bring his ships down the Atlantic from Britain, then cross the very southern lattitudes of the Indian Ocean, aiming for that entrance

---

[132] See Ian Watt, *The Rise of the Novel: Studies in Defoe, Richardson and Fielding*, Chatto & Windus, London, 1957, ch. vi.
[133] Blainey, *Captain Cook's Epic Voyage*, p. 46

to the South Seas—New Zealand. At Queen Charlotte Sound the vessels would make a fortnight's stop for this maintenance, a thorough cleaning and deck reorganisation. Using prevaling currents and winds, Cook would then have his ships sail the Pacific in an anti-clockwise arc, before halting at another safe anchorage to undertake the same procedures. On the second very long voyage he looped back to New Zealand twice, seeing to maintenance there each time. —This schedule which Cook worked to is why the *Adventure* had made that stop when men were lost in the Grassy Cove incident.

Of course, what much historical writing on ocean travel in Cook's day misses is noise. It takes a sailing journalist like Robert Mundle to emphasise the ever-present background sounds.[134] Waves slapped the hull, wind hummed and whistled through rigging, while the vessel produced a constant low cacaphony of wooden creaks, rhythmic knocks, and jingling of metal fittings. Sailing ships made these noises even in mild weather. Then there were the bells and whistles rung, rapped or blown at all hours to signal information or instructions, as well as verbal orders directly called by officers or shouted out by NCOs. There was also the clucks, crows, feathered flutters, grunts, snorts, squeals, farts, moos and stamping hooves of the livestock; then in daylight hours the hammering, sawing and banging about of the ship's carpenter, along with more domestic cleaning sounds as decks, stairs and walls were scraped, swabbed, scrubbed, brushed and polished daily.[135] Even lowly tars customarily made hearty noises as they laboured, using a cycle of work songs and rhythmic chants when performing assorted maritime tasks.

Midshipmans' journals do mention the recreational sounds. When off duty the crew often amused themselves by making music, singing and dancing. For this purpose sailors and marines

---

[134] Rob Mundle, *Cook: From Sailor to Legend*, ABC Books/Harper Collins, Sydney, 2013.
[135] In keeping with the 18th Century beliefs that disease was caused and conveyed by bad air ('maisma'), Cook insisted ships be aired out each day it wassafe to do so.

took fifes, hornpipes, drums, a form of fiddle, and a bagpipes on voyages; while the last expedition saw Cook (who was teaching himself the French Horn) attempt to organise a 'band', which elicited guarded remarks in some journals about off-key chaotic rehearsals. Besides sailors playing for themselves at sea when travelling, during Pacific stopovers they gave concerts before favoured native communities. On the second voyage chief Tu and his Tahitian retinue were delighted to be entertained by tars playing bagpipe music and dancing.[136] And on the third voyage Cook lead his ship's band in honking out several tunes at Tonga—'A most ludicrous performance,' Lieutenant Bligh recorded with momentary candour. 'C. Cook's Musicians or Musick was ill adapted'.[137]

Scrutinising once again those passages by McLynn and Salmond that have been found to be flawed, looking closely at what they wrote, at the sentences they laid out, both historians erred when vigilance and self-scrutiny were needed. Each was evidently tempted to repeat sensationalist details from the Marra text; and each succumbed. So errors crept in to their accounts, significant errors.

Overall Frank McLynn's biography of Cook is diligently researched; but, when handling the events Salmond claimed had occurred in Grassy Cove, he does not examine her sources. Instead, he paraphrases her version:

> just before dusk they came on around 200 Maoris gathered as if for a festivity. When they taunted the approaching boat party, Burney gave the order to open fire. Muskets, musketoons and wall-guns scythed through the packed ranks of Maoris, causing the survivors to run for cover in the trees. Once the beach was clear Burney reconnoitred and found the eyes, hearts, lungs, livers and entrails of their comrades roasting on fires. Reeling from the horror and fearing a counter-attack they re-embarked

---

[136] Salmond, *Trial of the Cannibal Dog*, pp. 199, 201-2.
[137] Beaglehole, *Journals of Cook*, vol. 3, pt. 1, p. 133.fn.

on the launch, first destroying the dozens of canoes drawn up on the beach ...[138]

Cutting corners in this way sees McLynn duplicate Salmond's defects, and add some of his own. Two beaches become one; firearms used by marines are incorrect; the number of Maoris and their canoes is grossly inflated. All is rounded off with a description of a wanton blood-bath as the marines' weapons "scythed through the packed ranks" of natives. A simple check of historical documents would have thrown doubt on this interpretation; because according to Burney, Furneaux, Bayly and Kahura it had been an ineffectual confrontation, with guns misfiring in the wet weather.[139] Kahura also boasted to Cook that no Maoris were wounded.

McLynn is not alone in taking Salmond on trust. Many historians now do the same, repeating her plotline without running a critical eye over her sources. One might expect more caution given her use of the Marra text which has long been viewed as unsafe. Yet it has not impeded broad acceptance of Salmond's analysis of what occurred. Having repeated her version, some authors include additional details to firm up their account of Burney's search. Take Robert Mundle in *Cook: From Sailor to Legend* (2013), who has Burney and the marines start firing at 'about 400 Maoris'.[140] Where this number came from is not indicated.[141] Was it made up? (Mundle had already claimed Rowe's party were killed because 'The Maoris were treating the Englishmen as invaders, an enemy, and the accepted custom of cannibalism prevailed'.[142] Again no source is given for this 'custom' which goes against what the Maoris, including Kahura himself, later told Cook about the conflict.)

---

[138] McLynn, *Master of the Seas*, pp. 224-5.
[139] The Marra text refrains from giving estimates of natives wounded or killed.
[140] Rob Mundle, *Cook: From Sailor to Legend*, ABC Books/Harper Collins, Sydney, 2013, p. 340.
[141] 'I have deliberately not provided the finer detail regarding sources,' the author writes before his endnotes. Mundle, *From Sailor to Legend*, pp. 447-8.
[142] Mundle, *From Sailor to Legend*, p. 341.

A complaint often levelled against academic historians is their writing can be colourless and dry. This cannot be said of Anne Salmond. Take her lively description of Burney's party conducting the search:

> By now it was almost dusk. They rowed the launch to Grass Cove, the adjacent bay, where they found canoes hauled up on the beach and hundreds of people gathered along the shore and on the hillside ... As the launch approached the beach some people began to taunt the sailors, calling out and gesturing for them to come ashore. Burney ordered his men to fire muskets and musketoons at will into the crowd. At the first volley the people seemed stunned; at the second volley they broke and ran for the trees, howling with fear and pain. The wall-guns were then loaded and fired, and the marines kept on shooting until nobody was left in sight. Burney left Fannin, the ship's master, to guard the boat, and searched the beach with a party of marines. They found one of the cutter's oars broken and stuck upright in the ground ... Dogs were chewing the discarded entrails of four or five men, and they found the eyes, hearts, lungs, livers and heads of their comrades, including the head of Furneaux's black servant, various feet, and Rowe's left hand (identified by its scarred forefinger) roasting on fires or scattered on the ground. Fannin called out that he could hear people shouting in the valley, perhaps preparing to attack, so they hastily gathered up some of these body parts and hurried back to the launch. They fired one last volley at a large crowd of people gathered on a hillside up the valley, and left the cove in darkness ...[143]

This is the work of a gifted story-teller, a writer who crafts sentences which make historical events 'come alive' for the reader. But Salmond at turns makes what should be a strength into a potential liability. Because in dramatising the past, she will insert evocative details that are assumed, not known. Blunt facts disappear amid verbal embroidery. And it is her small descriptive touches introduced to dramatise the 'story' being

---

[143] Salmond, *Trial of the Cannibal Dog*, p. 229.

related which lead to errors in geography, marine weaponry, and Maori numbers.

Salmond is not alone in playing loose with details in order to make the past seem vivid. History writers with a talent for story-telling need sometimes to practice restraint. For example, in *James Cook: The Story Behind the Man who Mapped the World* (2019) Peter FitzSimons will deliberately introduce phrases unknown in Cook's day. Like when he has Dr Monkhouse, who is checking sailors for syphilis, muse 'many of the crew are "pissing razor-blades" as the saying goes.'[144] An eighteenth century person would never speak like this. It is modern slang. With an exaggerated familiarity, FitzSimons also repeatedly refers to Lieutenant Clerke as 'Charlie' as if he was the author's acquaintance. But all the crew from the Captain to the tars addressed Charles Clerke as 'Mr Clerke'. It was the etiquette of the period.

Passing touches like these may be pardoned as literary licence which increase readability. What should not be excused is the occasional insertion of colourful details no historian could possibly know, in particular the fabrication of historic episodes. Like how FitzSimons adds a new episode to what occurred when, after the *Endeavour* was badly holed on a reef, Cook beached his vessel at a tidal river for repairs. That evening, in FitzSimons's narrative, the local Aborigines hold a Neighbourhood Watch meeting:

> they discuss the strange spirit and the ghostly men who arrived at *Wahalumbaal birri*, the river mouth of their land. The intruders are indeed strange and troubling. For they gorge on the fruits of this land, trample its grasses, disrespect its sacred sites and take more fish and turtles than they can possibly need. And they don't move on… The discussion goes well into

---

[144] Peter FitzSimons, *James Cook: The Story Behind the Man who Mapped the World*, Hatchette Australia, Sydney, 2019, p. 191. Razor Blade were first marketed by the Gillette company in 1880, a century after Cook's last voyage.

the starry night as they keep feeding the fire just what it needs, and no more.[145]

So runs his account of the meeting—but no one now knows what the Aborigines said and did. They left no record of Cook's stopover.

It is possible the Aboriginals held a gathering, indeed, they must have talked about the strangers. A differently inclined writer might have the Aborigines conduct religious rites, calling on creator spirits or ancestors for protection. But FitzSimons opts for a varient of a modern day Neighbourhood Watch meeting, even slipping in typical rumblings about how the strangers drain local resources.[146] (Through unexplained acts of clairvoyance FitzSimons also intermittently looks into various natives' minds and then relates what they were thinking.)

Fictional elements have manifestly entered not only accounts of how Burney's party responded when they found the remains of Rowe and his men. There are similar shortcomings to what is alleged to have occurred four years later when Burney was serving on Cook's third Pacific voyage. In an incident now known as 'The Trial of the Cannibal Dog', Lieutenant Burney reputedly allowed midshipmen to stage a mock trial in protest against Cook for not avenging the deaths at Grassy Cove.

In his 2011 biography of Cook, Frank McLynn summarises what the disgruntled midshipmen are said to have got up to:

> While Kahura went on deck to have his portrait painted by Webber, Omai bearded Cook in the Great Cabin and raged at him: 'Why do you not kill him? You tell me if a white man kills another in England he is hanged for it and yet you will not kill him, even though a great many of his own people would like that and it would be very good.' The general derision felt for Cook by his crew found expression on the *Discovery*, where James

---

[145] FitzSimons, *James Cook*, p. 333.
[146] At points FitzSimons feigns to read the Aborigines' thoughts, explaining they are alarmed the local marine environment is being put out of balance.

Burney connived at and encouraged an express act of defiance and contempt for his commander. Edward Riou had acquired a pariah dog from the Maoris, which was deeply unpopular as it liked to bite people. The midshipmen and master's mates staged a mock trial of this dog for cannibalism, convicted it, killed it, then cooked and ate it.[147]

McLynn relies here entirely on Anne Salmond's construction of events. He may cite a mixture of sources, but McLynn is uncritically repeating what appeared in her pioneering books—which combined anthropology with narrative history—*Between Worlds: Early Exchanges between Maori and Europeans* (1997) and *The Trial of the Cannibal Dog: Captain Cook in the South Seas* (2003). Having initially described what occurred in the dog episode in the earlier work, Salmond chose to feature it prominently with the latter book, an in-depth study of Cook's interactions with Pacific peoples. Besides using it for that book's attention catching title, the entire first chapter examined the unusual incident, offering a set of historical precedents. Much amused by the trial story, scholars accepted without checking Salmond's version of what took place and it soon transitioned into historical orthodoxy.

According to Salmond, Omai erupted when Cook instructed John Webber to make a portrait of Kahura, killer of the *Adventure*'s men. The sailors were likewise angered at the gesture, feeling their Captain was going too far. Insult had been added to injury. 'Although Clerke agreed that there was no purpose to be served by killing Kahura,' Salmond explains:

> Many of the sailors were of a mind with [Omai] and found their impotence galling. Burney spoke for them when he wrote: 'it seemed evident that many of them held us in great contempt and I believe chiefly on account of not avenging the affair of Grass Cove, so contrary to the principals by which

---

[147] McLynn, *Master of the Seas*, p. 293. McLynn makes two mistakes here. The portrait of Kahura was drawn, not painted, Webber doing so in his makeshift studio space in the Great Cabin, not on deck in open air.

they would have been actuated in the like case.' The scene was now set for the mock trial of the dog on board the *Discovery*. James Burney, the living witness of what had happened at Grass Cove and the ship's first lieutenant, was chafing at Cook's failure to act. The *Discovery* was Cook's consort ship, so the trial was staged at a safe distance from their commander. It was a marvellous way of letting Cook and Clerke know what the sailors (and some of their officers) thought of Maori cannibals, and how they ought to be handled.[148]

Continuing on, Salmond remarks the incident brings to mind 'The Great Cat Massacre,' a 1983 essay by the American historian Robert Darnton.[149] In it he argued that a purported incident in 1730s Paris, where two apprentices played a practical joke on their employer which ended in the killing of numerous cats, constituted a rebellion against harsh workplace relations imposed under France's *ancien régime*.[150] Having explained Darnton's piece, Salmond repeats at length the historical precedents he cited, using them for her own case. She then takes the metaphors further. Besides venting their anger at Cook, her argument runs, by eating a native dog they had from Maoris in trade, the midshipmen were symbolically enacting revenge against the Maori cannibals who ate the *Adventure*'s men. There are now psychological undertones to this meal, for it inverts what Burney reputedly saw on the beach (in the book's eleventh chapter): dogs had eaten the remains of butchered sailors, so sailors ate a dog as retaliation.[151]

There are difficulties here. Seemingly small, but significant ones nonetheless. Beginning with the sequence of events. Salmond has Kahura come aboard ship and meet Cook; the captain then takes Kahura into the Great Cabin where he instructs Webber to make Kahura's portrait; next an indignant Omai abuses Kahura, callng

---

[148] Salmond, *Trial of the Cannibal Dog*, p. 4.
[149] Robert Darnton, *The Great Cat Massacre and Other Episodes in French Cultural History*, Allen Lane, London, 1983.
[150] For criticisms of Darnton's essay see Richard Evans, *In Defence of History*, Granta, London, pp. 47-8.
[151] cf. Salmond, *Trial of the Cannibal Dog*, pp. 229-30.

for his death. It is after this Salmond has the midshipmen get up to mischief. But event do not follow that order in the journals of James Cook and David Samwell.[152] Each of them has Kahura arrive at the ship where an indignant Omai immediately abused him, calling for his death; Kahura next came aboard and met with Cook in the Great Cabin; then the captain instructed Webber to make Kahura's portrait. The change in sequence may be small, but ...

Other seamen's journals introduce more flaws. When Salmond's text is checked against the entry in James Burney's journal, nothing squares. Here in its entirety is what he wrote for this, his last day in New Zealand (with the sentence quoted by Salmond in italics):

> The New Zealanders of Queen Charlotte Sound were never so much among us as this time. The reason probably because they found more was got and on easier terms than ever before, for our folk were all so eager after curiosities and withall so much better provided than any other Voyage, that Traffick was greatly altered in favour of the Indians, a nail on the last Voyage purchasing more than an Axe or Hatchet now. before our departure Hatchets were slung under their Cloathes instead of Patows – They often appeared to have great Friendship for us, speaking sometimes in the most compassionate tone of Voice imaginable – but it not a little disgusted one to find all this Show of fondness interested and it constantly ended in begging. if gratified with their first demand they would immediately fancy something else, their expectations and importunities increasing in proportion as they had been indulged – We had instances of their quarrelling after having begged 3 things, because a fourth was denied them – *it seemed evident that many of them held us in great contempt and I believe chiefly on account of our not avenging the Affair of Grass Cove, so contrary to the principle by which they would have been actuated in the like Case.* another Cause might be their getting from us so many valuable things for which they gave the credit of their superior Cunning – as

---

[152] Beaglehole, *Journals of Cook*, vol. 3, pt.1, pp. 64-5; & vol. 3, pt.2, p. 1001.

an instance how much they trusted to our easiness one man did not scruple to acknowledge his being present and assisting at the killing and eating the Adventures people – No Beast can be more ravenous or greedy than a New Zealander. Nothing comes amiss; but no victuals was so highly relished by them as the rank Seal Blubber we bought from Kerguelens Land and which we boiled down here. so fond were they of this delicious food that some of our people who attended the Boiling have for the Skimming procured very substantial favour with the Ladies.[153]

Lieutenant Burney makes no reference here to midshipmen holding a mock trial of a dog, then eating it. Nor does he write of supporting defiant talk by sailors, of his frustration with either Cook or Clerke, or refer to Cook and Kahura meeting on the *Resolution*. He does not even mention Webber drawing the portrait of Kahura which Salmond insists greatly annoyed him. Both vessels were departing with the tide next morning, so we find Burney setting down final thoughts on a people he would not encounter again. No words are spent on Kahura, who, during the entire stopover, appears only briefly in Burney's notes.

Anne Salmond's sole reference point for Lieutenant Burney's thoughts—part of a sentence in his journal—has been taken out of context. The naval officer was writing on matters of trade with the Maoris. He may not have been pleased with the killers getting off, but there is not a scrap of evidence to suggest he was, as Salmond claims, 'chafing' to take action.

Where, then, does the dog incident come from? It is among a store of anecdotes much recited by Alexander Home. He had served as an adult midshipman on the *Discovery*, for a time acting as Master's Mate on that vessel. Some years later, after being left disabled by an accident aboard another navy ship, he retired on half-pay with the courtesy rank of Commander. Blind and near immobile, Home then spent his final years in the family home,

---

[153] Burney, *Journey on HMS Discovery*, vol.1, pp. 25-7.

craving an audience for his sea stories. 'He was full of narrative,' his son George remarked; but 'taking advantage of his blindness, we, his hopeful offspring, slipped quietly off, one by one, leaving, the old Commodore in his arm-chair.'[154] When served a generous meal, the agèd mariner would habitually reminisce on one prank aboard the *Discovery*:

> When we were in New Zealand, Neddy Riou, one of my messmates had got hold of a New Zealand dog, as savage a devil as the savages from whom he got it, and this same dog he intended to bring home to present to the Marchioness of Townsend, his patroness.[155] But one day, when Neddy was on shore on duty, a court-martial was held on the dog, and it was agreed *nem.con.* that, as the dog was of cannibal origin, and was completely a cannibal itself, having bit every one of us, and shewn every inclination to eat us alive if he could, that he should be doomed to death, and eat in his turn, we being short of fresh provisions at the time. The sentence was immediately executed, the dog cooked, dressed, and eat, for we could have eat a horse behind the saddle, we were all so confoundedly hungry; but, considering that Neddy had the best right to a share, we put past his portion in a wooden bowl, and by way of having some sport, we cut a hole in the dog's skin, and as Neddy came up the side, I popped his own dog's skin over his head with the tail hanging down behind, and the paws before. He looked the grin horrid, told us we were all a set of d—d cannibals, as bad as the New Zealanders we were amongst, and dived down below quite in the sulks.[156]

Salmond quotes this passage in full, although in neither of her books does she explain the source. Home's anecdote appears in the memoirs of his son, Lieutenant George Home, which were published in 1838—fifteen years after his father died. And far from being a statement made by Alexander Home and directly taken down, the passage is his son's effort to recite a yarn the

---

[154] George Home, *Memoirs of an Aristocrat, and Reminiscences of the Emperor Napoleon, by a midshipman of the Bellerophon*, London, Whittaker & co., 1838, p. 5.
[155] Home, *Memoirs of an Aristocrat*, p. 271.
[156] Ibid., pp. 271-2.

long deceased sailor used to tell. So not only must the dog story be reclassified as posthumously passed through a secondary source, but scholarly custom insists as an anecdote it be treated as corrupted. Because anecdotes evolve over time through retelling.

Home said the dog had been purchased by Midshipman Edward Riou in New Zealand. The two ships' stopped there once, remaining at Queen Charlotte Sound for the fortnight February 11 to 24, 1777. However, Home did not identify when and where during the voyage the dog eating incident occurred. The one evident clue is that the ship was running short of provisions. This eliminates Queen Charlotte Sound as a possibility, because, as Cook noted, Maoris offering fresh food in trade were a constant presence.[157] Canada, Alaska or Siberia seem more likely. It may even be the incident took place months after the death of Cook, in the long troubled journey from the Bering Sea to the Indian Ocean. As well, in his anecdote Home makes no mention of Kahura, of the meeting with Cook, of the *Adventure*'s crewmen, or of Lieutenant Burney. There are just no grounds to introduce them.

Returning to Salmond's account, she places the incident in New Zealand after Cook had forgiven Kahura. They met on the last day of the stopover, and the ship sailed the next morning. So the midshipmens' rebellious 'trial' could only have occurred after this late in the afternoon or evening of February 24. That day's entry in the journal of David Samwell, the surgeon's mate, records how Kahura arrived in the afternoon:

> While we lay at anchor here two or three large Canoes came to us in the Afternoon full of Men, they brought several Dogs to sell & we purchased a few of them for a Hatchet each, they had brought many Articles of Trade such as Ahoos [*patu*], green Images called Tigis [*tiki*], Stone Adzes &c., being desirous of getting a few more of our Hatchets before we left them. In

---

[157] Beaglehole, *Journals of Cook*, vol. 3, pt. 1, p. 61.

one of these Canoes was Kowura [Kahura] before mentioned; when Omai saw him he immediately went to Capt. Cook and begged that he wou'd give him permission to shoot him, saying that he was a very bad Man & that we ought to take revenge upon him for the Death of the Adventure's People. It is hardly necessary to mention that his Request was denied. The next Day Feby 25th we weighed and sailed out of Charlotte Sound ...[158]

So on the day in question Kahura and his kinsmen went to the ships to conduct trade, where, among other exchanges, they sold native dogs to the Europeans for a hatchet each. Was this when Midshipman Riou purchased the creature? Kahura next went aboard the *Resolution* and had his meeting with Cook in the great cabin, then sat for John Webber to make a portrait. According to Salmond's timeline, the other midshipmen now staged the 'trial' then killed and ate the expensive recently-acquired dog as a rebel gesture against Cook. And they did this aware of the workload awaiting them first thing the next day when the ships departed New Zealand.

Dates and times become so squeezed they will hardly mesh. Instead, it very much appears the sources used in Salmond's account have been selectively edited and a spurious pattern imposed on disconnected events. There are no grounds to doubt that the mock 'trial' of a dog did occur as described by Alexander Home, but it would have happened at a later point in the voyage. And far from being a bold political act motivated by what took place between Cook and Kahura, it was probably an instance of innocent fun among fatigued and underfed sailors trying to cope with a harsh situation.

---

[158] Beaglehole, *Journals of Cook*, vol. 3, pt. 2, p. 1001.

Pictorial Records

On visual information

John Webber, *The Death of Captain Cook*, 1782
(Engraving, 1784 Admirality edition)

Disregarding his own safety, a youthful Cook stands before hostile natives and gestures at his men to cease fire.

The Kahura portrait appears the least understood piece of evidence bearing on James Cook's relations with Pacific natives. Few historians dealing with Cook's voyages even mention this pencil drawing of February 24, 1777. Those who do acknowledge the portrait, pass over with minimal comment. The anthropologically inclined will pause to suggest Cook did not grasp the implications in having it made; because in honouring Kahura, a killer of sailors, the navigator would have 'lost face' in the opinion of local Maoris. But this highlights the need to delve into the uses native portraits were put to on those voyages, and—apart from art historians—writers of history just do not pause to consider that.

Due to their scientific purpose, in addition to customary naval records Cook's expeditions produced extensive written and visual materials on indigenous communities. The written accounts often highlight the interactive nature of encounters with natives, recording their reactions to things Europeans did in their presence. In contrast, the bulk of the related drawings focus upon subjects of anthropological or nautical interest, showing native huts, clothing, tools, handcrafts, tattoos and boats. Of course, There are drawings of natives going about normal activities, especially using boats and canoes, as well as fishing. There are also efforts to show physical differences, and how natives appear racially. And several dozen more works are actually portraits of individuals from Pacific communities.

Few portraits came from the *Endeavour* voyage. There were several reasons behind this. The artists aboard, Sydney Parkinson and Herman Spöring, were not skilled at rendering faces. Nor, due to a communication gap, were they often able to persuade uncomprehending natives to halt and pose for drawings. Instead they drew people in passing or at a distance, which resulted in sketched faces or expressions, rather than studied portraits. Besides, in the few instances where the artists did attempt more—

as in the pen and wash *Portrait of a New Zealand Man* now in the British Museum—due to the taxonomic inclinations of Joseph Banks, they seem to have been encouraged to show natives as generalised racial types, not individuals.[159] The diagram impulse is not distant.

Opportunity presented itself afresh on the second voyage. Historians have tended to over-intellectualise a qualitative difference evident across portrait drawings produced on the first and second voyages, suggesting William Hodges's work is less stilted because the artist was reconceptualising Pacific peoples.[160] There is a more straightforward explanation. Unlike his predecessors on the *Endeavour* who were illustrators drilled in the use of pencil and pen, Hodges was a trained artist with a firm grounding in the life class. He could use chalk or charcoal to precisely render a human face, bringing pastels on the voyage to do so. Added to this, Cook himself made an effort to persuade natives he befriended to pose for portrait drawings.

George Forster gives a vivid account of how the first drawings came about when Cook initially returned to New Zealand in spring 1773. At Dusky Bay on April 7, a small party from the *Resolution* took the cutter ashore. When a Maori family appeared on the beach, the expedition's leader was elated:

> Captain Cook went to the head of the boat, called to him [the male Maori] in a friendly manner, and threw him his own and some other handkerchiefs, which he would not pick up. The captain then taking some sheets of white paper in his hand, landed on the rock unarmed, and held the paper out to the native. The man now trembled very visibly, and having

---

[159] No portraits of Australian Aboriginals were produced on Cook's *Endeavour* expedition, the artists being unable to persuade any Aboriginal to pose on their few, very brief visits to the continent. John Webber was able to attempt a portrait of a Tasmanian Aboriginal after the *Resolution* made a short stop to obtain water on the third Pacific expedition.

[160] Admittedly I rely here on my own background teaching life drawing in art schools. Any drawing teacher will point to clear differences in the respective artists' training, and competence. Hodges's professional skill stands out across his drawings, even in his handling of chalk and charcoal.

exhibited strong marks of fear in his countenance took the paper: upon which captain Cook coming up to him, took hold of his hand, and embraced him, touching the man's nose with his own, which is their mode of salutation. His apprehension was by this dissipated, and he called to the two women, who came and joined him, while several of us landed to keep the captain company. A short conversation ensued, of which little was understood on both sides, for want of a competent knowledge of the language. Mr. Hodges immediately took sketches of their countenances, and their gestures shewed that they clearly understood what he was doing; on which they called him tóä-tóä, that term being probably applicable to the imitative arts.[161]

Over following days the artist made several full figure sketches of the same Maoris standing within the landscape. —Back in London, Hodges would integrate those figures into oil paintings of the scene.

On May 18 the *Resolution* reached Ship Cove, its former anchorage in Queen Charlotte Sound, prompting excitement and celebration among resident Maoris. Even as the crew set about ship's maintenance, Cook instructed Hodges to make portrait drawings of natives who caught his eye. The artist wasted no time in bringing them on board for sittings that day. Anders Sparrman describes the bafflement of the first young woman to be drawn:

> Language difficulties at first gave rise to a misunderstanding between the girl and the painter, for she, having been well paid to go down into the saloon, imagined that she ought to give satisfaction, in the way she understood it, as soon as possible in return for her gift, perhaps she had previous experience with our sailors? She was astonished when signs were made for her to sit on a chair; such novel ways of doing things struck her as absurd, but she promptly volunteered a prone position upon the chair for the painter and his companion. To her

---

[161] Forster, Voyage Round the World, vol 1, pp. 137-8; Joppien & Smith, *Art of Cook's Voyages*, vol. 2, pp. 26-7.

further surprise she was eventually put in a correct position, just sitting on the chair with nothing to do, whereupon, to the wonderment and entertainment of herself and the two savages with her, she quickly saw her likeness in a red chalk drawing ...[162]

Fascinated to watch Hodges draw these works, the 'experimental gentlemen' aboard—George and Johann Forster, Anders Sparrman and William Wales—were sympathetic to studied portraits which humanised Pacific natives. Two days later the artist had a mixed native group in the great cabin, intending to draw some. George Forster explains what set the naturalists wanting images of these Maoris:

> Several of the people were invited into the cabin, where Mr Hodges applied himself to sketch the most characteristic faces, while we prevailed on then to sit still for a few moments, keeping their attention engaged, by a variety of trifles which we shewed, and some of which we presented to them. We found several expressive countenances among them, particularly some old men, with grey or white beards; and some young men, with amazingly bushy hair, which hung wildly over their faces, and increased their natural savage looks.[163]

It was initially hoped the artist would record at least three samples of both male and female natives of certain ages at each island group. But, as the naturalists socialised with natives, the project gradually shifted from compiling information on Islander physiognomy to portraying individuals. Flattered to be drawn, natives willingly complied, although the names of persons drawn were not recorded.

Of course, from the 1750s chalk pastel was the preferred medium of portraitists seeking to evoke a sitter's identity. It was felt a proficient rendering in chalk did not just convey the subject's likeness. It suggested their temperament, which is why skilled

---

[162] Anders Sparrman, *A Voyage Round the World with Captain James Cook in HMS Resolution*, London, 1944, p. 44; Smith, *Imagining the Pacific*, p. 83.
[163] Forster, *Voyage Round the World*, vol 1, p. 213; Smith, *Imagining the Pacific*, p. 100.

artists used a precise preliminary chalk drawing as reference when they painted a likeness in oils. So it is no wonder that on Tahiti the naturalists appeared now to want Hodges's portraits to give a sense of what the natives were like *as individuals*. Forster writes as much when recalling a balmy day (August 21) near Vaitepiha Bay, where an extended family welcomed into their large hut the Forsters, father and son, William Hodges and a midshipman. 'They desired us to sit down,' he recalls, and a halting conversation ensued. 'Charmed with the picture of real happiness, which was thus exhibited before us, Mr. Hodges filled his port-folio with several sketches, which will convey to future times the beauties of a scene, of which words give but a faint idea.'[164] The natives were delighted by the images: 'While he was drawing, all the natives looked on with great attention, and were highly pleased to find out the resemblance between his performances and different persons among them.'[165]

Not long after this Cook instructed Hodges to make a sensitive portrait of 'Otoo' (Tu) the *arii nui* (leading chieftain) of Tahiti's Pare region, adjacent to Matavai Bay. The finished work was to be partly an act of diplomacy, signalling his esteem for the tribal leader, partly a mark of their developing friendship. Over the course of the voyage it would be followed by similarly inclined 'respectful' portraits of 'Potatow' (Patatau), the *arii* (chief) of Punaauia in Tahiti, of 'Tainamai' (Tynai-mai), the daughter of *arii* Orio of Raiatea, and of 'Hatago' (Otãgo), *arii* of Tongatapu. As well Hodges thrice drew 'Oedidee' (Hitihiti), a youth from Bora Bora who travelled for several months aboard the *Resolution* on its Pacific circuit around New Zealand, Easter Island and Tahiti. A record was kept of the sitter's name for each of these renderings.

In July 1775, upon returning to Britain, William Hodges delivered to the Admiralty all the paintings and drawings he had

---
[164] Forster, *Voyage Round the World*, vol 1, p. 292; Joppien & Smith, *Art of Cook's Voyages*, vol. 2, pp. 58-9.
[165] Ibid.

made on the voyage, including the portrait drawings. Thirty three of his native portraits have survived, while engravings indicate another three portrait drawings he made have been lost over the centuries.[166] For reasons that are unclear, when the choice of book illustrations was made only a third (or fourteen) of these fine renderings were selected for reproduction. Most of the original portrait sketches are in red chalk on loose sheets of paper measuring 21¼ x 14¾ in (54 x 37.5 cm), although several are in charcoal with touches of white chalk. All the renderings meticulously represent the sitter's head and shoulders. The artist is careful throughout not to stylise musculature or features. Apart from a cloak reaching the neck on some natives, attire is not shown. Several portraits do have natives wearing jewellery of shell, carved bone and feathers. Those Hodges drew on Easter Island show the natives with all ornament removed from their ears, thereby revealing their sizable ear piercings and very elongated lobes.

There was intense interest when word circulated in London that Hodges had made so many fine drawings of Pacific natives. Private viewings of his portrait studies were arranged for members of the Royal Society. By coincidence, two months prior to the *Resolution's* return in mid-1775, Sir Joshua Reynolds, the president of the Royal Academy, had shown in its Spring exhibition his oil painting of Omai the Tahitian mentioned above.[167] Portraiture was at its peak during this phase of British culture, full length portraits taking pride of place in the Royal Academy's annual exhibit. As the cornerstone of private patronage, such pictures were vehicles

---

[166] The greater number of Hodges's portrait drawings are held in the collection of the National Library of Australia, Canberra, with much of the remainder in the collection of the Mitchell Library, State Library of NSW, Sydney. Several original portraits are also held by the Public Archives of Canada, Ottowa, as well as one each by the Alexander Turnbull Library, Wellington, New Zealand, the British Museum, London and the Peabody Library, Salem, Massachussetts.

[167] Reynold's portrait of Omai is customarily dated as being painted over 1775-76, however Omai's biographer, E.H.McCormick, has found that the full length formal work was initially shown in the Royal Academy during Spring 1775. McCormick, *Omai, Pacific Envoy*, p. 174.

chiefly for social display and aggrandisement, being highly theatrical and idealised. Accordingly, the academician's canvas showed Omai before a palm in an imagined tropical landscape, and standing bare-footed in the classical pose used to indicate diplomacy. The native was clad in linen robes, gathered about his arms in a patrician manner, with a white turban placed on his head: as the art historian Joseph Burke observed, 'his spurious Tahitian garb evokes the Rajah and the Roman Senator.'[168] In keeping with Reynolds's own theories of beauty, Omai's facial features—his broad nose, for instance, and stiff uneven hair—were considerably altered, being made to look more Grecian. The only seeming concession to the Tahitian's real appearance were tattoos shown encircling his right wrist and clustered on the back of his left hand.

When they saw Hodges's factual renderings, the learned gentlemen of the Royal Society were astounded. The artist depicted Pacific natives free of theatrical pomp and stylistic formula. The response was overwhelmingly positive, and Hodges was encouraged to develop certain renderings into formal portraits in oils. But the artist's creative ambitions lay elsewhere. He aspired to establish himself as a landscapist, and planned to work up several Pacific view paintings and Polynesian scenes. His hope was to see them hung in the Royal Academy (they were selected for inclusion in its 1776 Spring show[169]). Hodges therefore had no artistic aspirations for his portrait drawings, being satisfied enough to see engraved copies made of certain

---

[168] Smith, *Imagining the Pacific*, p. 175; Joseph Burke, *English Art 1714-1800*, Oxford, 1976, p. 205.

[169] If public interest was high in 1776, the critical reception for more of Hodges's Polynesian paintings shown the following year was rocky. Some viewers were perturbed by his efforts to convey the intense light, considering the works much too brightly coloured, and the painterly qualities of his pictures came in for censure: as a hostile critic wrote, 'It is surprising, however, that a man of Mr Hodges's genius should adopt such a ragged mode of colouring; his pictures all appear as if they were unfinished, and as if the colours were laid on the canvas with a skewer.' *London Packet or New Lloyd's Evening Post*, 25 April 1777; Joppien & Smith, *Art of Cook's Voyages*, vol. 2, p. 85.

images for use as illustrations in the official book on the second voyage.

Nevertheless, following the Royal Society's viewings, and as a probable corrective to Reynolds's very contrived portrait, William Hodges did paint in oils a close up portrait of Omai. This near life-size image on a modest oval-shaped canvas, was commissioned by John Hunter, the distinguished surgeon and anatomist, who wanted an accurate representation of the Tahitian's head for use in comparative physiognomy, and trusted only Hodges to get it right.[170] The artist ran it off in a single session in his Mayfair studio.[171] With deftly handled brush, this intimate oil has many of the same naturalistic qualities as his portrait drawings: a Polynesian of around twenty years of age with warm brown eyes and a broad muscular face looks toward the viewer. This work was included when the committee made a selection of Hodges's native portraits to reproduced in the book on Cook's second Pacific voyage.

The artistic agenda changed once again when the next Pacific expedition departed Britain in July 1776. Cook had fresh plans and a new artist in John Webber. Few portraits of natives would be made on the voyage, most of them being quite unidentifiable.[172]

Still, the Captain did hang in his cabin a portrait drawing of a Polynesian chief.[173] Whether this was a work by Hodges from the previous expedition, or a fresh rendering by Webber, is unknown. Either way, what Cook intended by so prominently displaying a native portrait must be asked. Among crew members it probably served to emphasise their Captain's respect and liking for Pacific

---

[170] The portrait is now in the collection of the Royal College of Surgeons. Joppien & Smith, *Art of Cook's Voyages*, vol. 2, pp. 64-5.

[171] Hodges's studio is recorded as being in Queen Street, Mayfair.

[172] At each landfall Webber made careful full-figure drawings of at least one man and one woman for his reference when devising multi-figure compositions. Smith, *Imagining the Pacific*, p. 74; Joppien & Smith, *Art of Cook's Voyages*, vol. 2, p. 19.

[173] Joppien & Smith, *Art of Cook's Voyages*, vol. 2, p. 20; Beaglehole, *Journals of Cook*, op.cit., vol. 3, pt. 1, p. 69.

peoples. Likewise the image showed natives who came aboard the esteem he held their chiefs in, while the historians Rudiger Joppien and Bernard Smith wonder if it may also have been 'a means of cultivating friendship.'[174]

John Webber was not burdened with sketching multiple portraits of natives at each landfall, yet there were at least four occasions when Cook instructed him to draw tribal leaders. The first to sit was Kahura. The Maori requested a portrait following his signal meeting with the navigator in which the pair set aside past troubles. The chief was surely aware that on his travels Cook had portraits drawn of chiefs both locally, and across Polynesia, as a mark of his respect and friendship. So having this work made amounted to an act of diplomacy in the eyes of local Maoris, the portrait serving to seal the 'peace agreement' between Cook and Kahura.

The others singled out for portraits on the voyage included Paulaho, an *arii* of Tahiti, Poedua, another daughter of Orio, the *arii* of Raiatea, as well as Tu, the *arii nui* of Tahiti who had already been drawn by Hodges.[175] (If not annotated, a fine drawing of an *arii* from Bora Bora is probably 'Opoony' [Puni].) In each instance Cook assured the sitter this was a special sign of his own respect and friendship—the artist later related the conversation Cook and Charles Clerke had with Tu, and how they stressed the portrait would be a permanent record of his own status and authority:

> Otoo by the Captain's particular desire, sat to Mr Webber, in order to furnish such memorial of his features, as might serve for the subject of a complete whole length picture, on the return of the ship to England. When the portrait was finished and Otoo was informed that no more sittings would be necessary, he anxiously enquired of Captain Cook, and Captain Clerke, what might be the particular meaning and purpose of the painting. He was informed, that it would be kept by Captain Cook, as a

---

[174] Joppien & Smith, *Art of Cook's Voyages*, vol. 2, p. 20.
[175] Ibid., p. 19.

perpetual memorial of his person, his friendship, and the many favours received from him.[176]

Tu requested a pencil portrait of Cook in exchange. The navigator agreed to this, and a drawing in a lockable wooden box was presented to the chief. Henceforth Tu would use this as a status symbol and mark of his power. Years later, when the *HMS Lady Penrhyn* visited Tahiti in winter 1788, Tu showed this cherished image of Cook to the ship's officers: 'Notwithstanding so much time had elapsed since the picture was drawn,' Lieutenant Watts wrote, 'it had received no injury, and [we] were informed that O'too always carried it with him wherever he went.'[177]

More scientific information was obtained upon each of Cook's Pacific expeditions than on any previous oceanic journey. Every day of a voyage saw different personnel take observations in their assigned field, measuring and recording; meanwhile others aboard were engaged in analysing, computing, tabulating and cataloguing information gathered. As a consequence Cook's voyages prompted new developments in documented evidence. Besides charts, numerical data and written descriptions, it was evident a pictorial record was needed.

Visual artists were expected to show with graphic precision what might not be adequately portrayed by other means. The results were far-reaching as assorted branches of scientific illustration were developed. For instance, the taxonomic drawings produced on the *Endeavour* expedition by Sydney Parkinson (which were firmly anchored in Linnean analysis) reconfigured the very practice of botanical illustration, setting a benchmark that those who came afterward strove to meet.

Subsequent Pacific expeditions saw increasing attention focused on anthropology and ethnography. The artists recruited—

---

[176] No author, *Voyage of Governor Phillip to Botany Bay*, London, 1789, pp. 293-4; Smith, *Imagining the Pacific*, p. 107.
[177] *Voyage of Governor Phillip*, pp. 233-4; Smith, *Imagining the Pacific*, p. 108.

William Hodges on the second voyage, then John Webber assisted by John Ellis on the third—were to deliver observational drawings of native peoples engaged in routine activities, as well as images of their villages and handcrafts. Cook personally selected visual artists, explaining what he required them to portray; as he wrote of preparations for the final voyage: 'Mr Webber was pitched upon, and engaged to embark with me, for the express purpose of supplying the unavoidable imperfections of written accounts, by enabling us to preserve, and to bring home, such drawings of the most memorable scenes of our transactions...'[178] (That said, both artists found themselves attempting a new kind of view painting anchored in *plein aire* observation, rather than adhering to the pictorial and stylistic formulas of the Royal Academy.[179])

Even as Cook's third expedition was wending through Polynesia, back in London the scientific value of those pictures of natives was challenged. Work towards the book reporting on that expedition had been proceeding well, with William Hodges using wash drawings he made at certain inhabited islands to design then paint on paper several events in the South Seas.[180] The engraver John Keyes Sherwin made prints of these pieces so they might appear among the book's illustrations. But George Forster, one of the naturalists from the second voyage, complained that the engraver had altered imagery and thereby rendered certain illustrations scientifically inaccurate.

Forster took exception to *The Landing at Middleburgh*.[181] This composition portrayed Cook arriving at Eua in Tonga, and being greeted by natives. Forster had seen the initial oil painting and commended it for, among other things, its anthropological accuracy. In the work William Hodges most carefully rendered the apparel, jewellery, hair styles and body markings of the

---

[178] J. Cook & J. King, *A Voyage to the Pacific Ocean*, London, 1784, vol. 1, p. 5; Smith, *Imagining the Pacific*, p. 73.
[179] Joppien & Smith, *Art of Cook's Voyages*, vol. 2, p. 71.
[180] Ibid., p. 70.
[181] Ibid., pp. 70-3.

natives. Sherwin did not strictly copy these details when he engraved the print version. In keeping with fashionable taste, Forster complained, the engraver had altered the appearance of Polynesian natives so that they 'exhibited to our eyes the pleasing forms of antique figures and draperies, instead of those Indians of which we wished to form an idea.' He went on:

> The connoisseur will find Greek contours and features in this picture which have never existed in the South Sea. He will admire an elegant flowing robe which involves the whole head and body, in an island where women very rarely cover the shoulders and breast; and he will be struck with awe and delight by the figure of a divine old man, with a long white beard, though all the people of Ea-oowhee shave themselves with muscle shells.[182]

Hodges may have prepared works of scrupulous verisimilitude, yet when Sherwin made the prints he gently spruced up scenes and figures with an eye on accepted stylistic customs. It appeared the claims of high-brow culture had taken precedence over the claims of Enlightenment science. This undermined the purpose of taking an artist on the expedition and having him record native activities. One could not even defend the printed image for its value as reportage, for it did not document visually what had taken place.

One of the expedition's astronomers, William Wales, rallied to the defence. He contended Forster was over-reacting. Citing works he had watched Hodges render on-the-spot in the Pacific, Wales felt that where changes occurred they were mostly slight. And he wondered if claimed alterations to Polynesian physiognomy were more a matter of interpretation, being not as pronounced as the naturalist claimed, adding that some natives he and Hodges encountered were bearded.

Comparing the original drawings against the engraved

---

[182] Forster, *Voyage Round the World*, vol. 1, pp. 427-8; Joppien & Smith, *Art of Cook's Voyages*, vol. 2, pp. 72-3; Smith, *Imagining the Pacific*, p. 72.

illustrations, professors Rüdiger Joppien and Bernard Smith tested these claims in the 1980s when they catalogued the drawings made on Cook's voyages. The historians found there sometimes was creative licence to Sherwin's engravings, as evident with the portrait of Otāgo, chief of Tongatapu, reproduced in Cook's work on the second voyage. Hodges's chalk drawing shows the young chief with wisps of hair on his chin, a bare chest and shoulders.[183] But Otāgo's chin is shaded in the illustration, and he is clothed in classical draperies gathered at the shoulder.[184] The engraving also has Otāgo clasp a spike nail over his hair in a symbolic gesture of greeting.

Checking all illustrations, irrespective of engraver, the two historians found changes were mostly minimal, as William Wales contended at the time. Typical of this is the portrait of Tynai-mai, daughter of Oreo, the chief of Raiatea. The drawing by Hodges had fixed on the adolescent's head, with her neck and shoulders concealed by a suggested stiff cloth.[185] For the book illustration, the engraver copied the rendered face with care, gave her girlish hair more body and curl, then changed the vague cloth into draperies which Oreo holds against herself with a slender hand.[186]

Nevertheless, in the mid-1770s Forster's comments struck a chord in intellectual circles. A broader readership also realised the anthropological purpose of works made by artists, how what they produced needed to be aligned with the aims of a scientific expedition, even though could be at odds with stylistic conventions. Henceforth great care was needed when the illustrations were engraved, with observational drawings of native peoples being copied most meticulously.

---

[183] Hodges made the chalk drawing on October 9, 1773. 2.75. Joppien & Smith, *Art of Cook's Voyages*, vol. 2, pp. 68, 183.

[184] Joppien & Smith, op. cit., p. 68. The illustration is Plate XL in Cook's work.

[185] Hodges made the chalk drawing on September 10, 1773. 2.71, Joppien & Smith, op. cit., p. 179.

[186] 2.71A, Joppien & Smith, op.cit., p. 180.

The result would be the superb plates faithfully copied from John Webber's compositions, and then printed for the atlas of Cook's third voyage. However, there was a single exception when that book was prepared. On instructions from the Admiralty a meagre illustration showing the navigator's death was included. Made up by the commercial artist D.P.Dodd, the engraving depicted natives stripping a European corpse on a beach as distant marines fire rifles from a launch.[187] The small image did not sit well amid Webber's careful pictures of the Pacific. Dodd's palm trees were ornamental clichés, while his Hawaiian natives were bearded Europeans in Hellenistic draperies. Realising the disparity, the Admiralty was forced at a late hour to enter an agreement with the artists John Webber and William Byrne for an immense illustration which has since become the most reproduced historical image to come down to us from James Cook's voyages.

On April 12, 1781, in the evening edition of the *St James Chronicle,* London society's newspaper of choice, a notice appeared among the commercial columns advertising properties for sale, and new books of sermons. 'Mr. Webber, the Artist,' it announced, 'who attended Captain Cook during his last Voyage, and who is employed by the Admiralty in finishing his Drawings for the Purpose of their being engraved to accompany the History of that Voyage, which will be published by Authority, intends shortly to deliver Proposals for publishing by Subscription, an Engraving of the Death of that great Navigator.'[188] The master engraver Francesco Bartolozzi R.A. would be incising each figure in the crowded scene, with William Byrne, a specialist in landscape prints, seeing to the overall tropical setting. Both had been praised for engraving the illustrations in Cook's works on his previous voyages. They would now reproduce a drawing 'taken on the Spot; the Landscape is from Nature; and the

---

[187] See Smith, *Imagining the Pacific,* pp. 232-3, illus 202.
[188] *St James Chronicle or the British Evening Post,* Apr. 12-14, 1781, p. 4. The advertisement was also carried in the newspaper's subsequent issue of Apr. 14-17

Circumstances of that most unfortunate Event (of which Mr. Webber was an Eye-Witness) are told with the utmost Fidelity."[189] Advance subscriptions for this exceptional work were being offered by Webber and Byrne—a customary practice used by artists and printmakers to fund costly publications.

The project was surely influenced by the commercial success of a print portraying the death of another British worthy, General Wolfe in the Battle of Quebec. Over eighteen months this subject had been painted by the rival academicians Benjamin West and Edward Penny. Their pictures were shown to public acclaim in the Royal Academies of 1770 then 1771. West delayed in releasing an engraving of his work for six years, whereas a fetching mezzotint of Penny's piece was published within six months of the exhibition by the Fleet Street map and print seller Robert Mayer.[190] It shows two grenardiers and a colonel anxiously attending Wolfe, who has slumped on a rocky wilderness outcrop, as the distant British army advances in smart formation.[191] Issued in January 1772 the print enjoyed remarkable commercial longevity. Mayer and his business partner, John Bennett, cut the plate down to just the figure group in October 1779, and issued costly hand-coloured prints of this smaller version.[192] So when Webber arrived back from his Pacific voyage, he would have found Penny's image of

---

[189] *St James Chronicle or the British Evening Post*, Apr. 12-14, 1781, p. 4.

[190] Richard Houston rocked the mezzotint's plate. The plate dimensions are not precisely known, but it was slightly less than 17 x 20 in (42.8 x 50 cm), so it was close to the size of Webber's finished drawing. The print of Penny's work was published by Robert Sayer of 53 Fleet Steet on January 1, 1772. William Woolley engraved the print of West's picture, which was published by Philip Hadrell of Leicester Square in 1776.

[191] West's now more famous picture was composed as an allegory. In the centre foreground the dying general is attended by three grenadiers at the edge of the energetic battle. Around clusters of people silently watch the death, including a soldier bearing the British flag, a native Indian and frontiersmen while a grenardier approaches with the French pennant captured from the French governor. In the distance beyond the smoke of battle we can see (to the right) a naval war fleet attacking Quebec, and (to the left) the besieged Quebec about to be liberated from the French.

[192] The coloured mezzotint was published by Robert Sayer and John Bennett on October 10, 1779. Again the dimensions of the plate are not precisely known, but it was slightly less than 14 x 10 in (35.5 x 25 cm).

heroic self-sacrifice still selling on the London print market and commanding a good price.

The Death of Captain Cook was another of John Webber's skilfully contrived composites. He had not seen the killings on the beach that morning, for he was aboard the *Resolution* working up a picture when the clash occurred. So the artist used what Lieutenant Phillips and his marines said when they returned to the ship, designing a dramatic picture by drawing the Hawaiian setting then setting figures in place within it. No drawing for the picture was among the works Webber delivered to the Admiralty after the expedition, so presumably it was mostly devised in his London studio.[193] Still, as indicated in the advertisement, in early 1781 Lord Sandwich appointed Webber to the committee to oversee production of illustrations for the forthcoming book of Cook's third Pacific voyage.[194] So the Admiralty was well aware that he had a print project underway.

In mid-May the *St James Chronicle* announced Webber had now completed his picture *The Death of Captain Cook*.[195] It could be viewed by prospective subscribers at William Byrne's print workshop at Great Titchfield Street, Fitzrovia (Bartolozzi's workshop was next door).[196] Over following days the same notice appeared in other newspapers.[197] They added that printer's materials were being delivered, and work upon the engraving was soon to commence, with subscriptions for the print currently being taken at London's busiest map and print seller, Boydell's of

---

[193] Joppien & Smith, *Art of Captain Cook's Voyages*, vol. 3, p. 121.

[194] The committee overseeing illustrations comprised Lord Sandwich, Sir Joseph Banks, Philip Stevens, the secretary to the Admiralty, Dr John Douglas, editor of the Atlas, Captain James King, Cook's co-author, Alexander Dalrymple, the hydrographer, James Stuart for the publishers Strahan and Cadell, and John Webber the artist. Joppien & Smith, *Art of Cook's Voyages*, vol. 3, p. 161.

[195] *St James Chronicle or the British Evening Post*, May 19-22.

[196] Byrne's workshop was at 79 Great Titchfield Street. The commercial premises of 'Bartolozzi & Co' moved into 81 Great Titchfield Street in late 1780 where it doubled as a print seller and workshop. Francesco Bartolozzi was so successful he was able also to keep a residence elsewhere.

[197] *Morning Herald*, Apr. 18, 1781; *Morning Chronicle*, May 4, 1781.

Cheapside, as well as Byrne's workshop, and, of course, Webber's studio on Bolsover St, off Oxford Street.[198] The prospects were positive. Having the entrepreneurial John and Josiah Boydell in on the project ensured wide promotion in Britain, and links with eager print sellers on the Continent.[199]

Now in Sydney's Mitchell Library, what is believed to be the unsigned original work is in pen, wash and watercolour on a sheet of paper measuring 14 x 21 in (35.7 x 53.5 cm).[200] In reality Cook and the marines had been surrounded by a mass of Hawaiians: one could not possibly see into the mêlée. However, like a theatrical performance upon a grand stage, *The Death of Captain Cook* is arranged along a frontal plane.[201] The setting is a tranquil landscape. Hazy clouds float above, a sandy beach opens to the left, palm trees and vegetation form a loose screen slightly back, allowing a glimpse of conical native huts, with mountains rising behind. A hoard of athletic natives has overrun a group of Europeans at the shoreline.

A conspicuously youthful James Cook commands the composition. Where ever the eye wanders it is lead back to his heroic figure. In contrast to the dark Hawaiians, the navigator is attired in white clothing—even his uniform jacket is an undyed white, not regulation naval blue—while the engraving uses the trunks of the largest palms in the picture's centre to point in a 'V'-like arrow at the Captain. Standing at centre stage, Cook strikes a dramatic pose. He does not lead the fight, indeed, bearing in his left hand an unused and bayonet-less musket, he represents a pocket of calm amid the violence. Looking to pictorial left, the navigator gestures

---

[198] Webber's studio was at 3 Bolsover Street, adjacent ot 312 Oxford Street. Besides their map and print shot at 90 Cheapside, John and Josiah Boydell were about to open an exhibition space, Shakespeare Gallery, on Pall Mall.

[199] Peter Ackroyd, *Blake*, Vintage, London, 1995, p. 97.

[200] Mitchell Library PXD59, f.1; Joppien & Smith, *Art of Captain Cook's Voyages*, vol. 3, p. 536., cat.3.304.

[201] All is rationally proportioned. The distant shore sits a third of the way up the composition; the mountains are sloped at a thirty degree angle; and with a rocky outcrop jutting across from the right, that foreground beach sets the edge of a disguised stage.

with his outstretched right arm and calls to a launch off-shore. He is unaware of a native warrior behind him, who is about to plunge a dagger into his neck.

Lieutenant Phillips, his hat fallen on the sand, has been pushed to the ground before Cook. From a half-sitting position this officer fires his musket at an assailant trying to club him. Around Phillips imperilled marines fight for their lives. One jabs at natives with his bayonet, another rating is being held down and knifed, a third lies dead. To the left of this skirmish three marines retreat at the water's edge, two more struggle in waves, while Lieutenant Williamson and several tars in two crammed boats shoot at the native crowd from the water.

John Webber and William Byrne jointly published the print *The Death of Captain Cook* under the Copyright Act on January 1, 1782.[202] It was a handsome image engraved into a plate measuring 17 x 23 in (43 x 58 cm), slightly larger than the pen and wash drawing. Bartolozzi, who was now Engraver to the King, had incised the figures with precision while Byrne deftly handled scenic details as well as seeing to overall production of what was a quality edition. Intended to be framed and displayed as a picture, the print was too large to be bound in a book. Following John Boydell's practice for the European print market, each copy came with a brief single page description explaining the scene and identifying figures, the text appearing in English on one side, and in French on the recto.[203]

---

[202] Under a 1767 amendment to the Copyright Act (1735), engravers held copyright of their works within Britain for twenty-eight years after publication. So every print carried its publication date, and the publisher's name and address. On the Act see Vic Gatrell, *The First Bohemians: Life and Art in London's Golden Age*, Allen Lane, London, 2013, pp. 109-110; Jenny Uglow, *Hogarth: A Life and a World*, Faber & Faber, London, 1997, pp. 268-70.

[203] In 1782 Webber and Byrne pressed the Admiralty to be allowed to visit Paris to obtain paper for the illustrations in the Atlas of Cook's third voyage. Presumably they would discuss Continental Rights to the *Death of Cook*, as well. But the trip was cancelled due to Joseph Banks, who contacted a Parisian bookseller about both the paper, and negotiating associated Rights. Joppien & Smith, *Art of Captain Cook's Voyages*, vol. 3, p. 165.

The Death of Captain Cook was a unique case. The original work the print was copied from had not been formally exhibited. Indeed, unlike William Hodges before him, John Webber had not developed his initial pencil and watercolour picture into a large oil painting which he then displayed in the Royal Academy's spring show. Instead Webber's composition was all along intended to be known and perceived by the public as a print, that is, as a mechanically reproduced work of art. But being unexhibited, Webber's composition was not the subject of art reviews and critical commentary—by seeming to exist solely as an engraving, it attracted no press discussion of its pictorial value.

Fleet Street may have been silent. Yet Webber's print portrayed an important event; in fact, it would be the only view of Hawaii and its peoples in public circulation until such time as the book on Cook's voyage came out. So there was keen interest in seeing this fastidiously detailed engraving. Subscribers were prevailed upon to show the striking print at private gatherings where guests looked, marvelled, talked.

A second edition of *The Death of Captain Cook* appeared nearly two years later. The first plate was beginning to show wear due to the number of impressions purchased by collectors wanting to own the work. So a newly engraved print was published by Webber and Byrne in January 1784.[204] The composition was unchanged, although there were slight adjustments in the degree of stylisation and tonal values: very slightly the new engraving was less Italianate, and overall it was a more shady work with the Polynesians portrayed having a darker skin tone.

Webber had taken risks with his picture. But endorsement, of sorts, was about to occur with the exhibition of an immense oil painting depicting heroic sacrifice. In May 1784 the rising artist John Singleton Copley rented the Great Room in the Hay Market where he displayed *The Death of Major Peirson, 6 January 1781*.[205]

---

[204] Published under the Act on January 1, 1784, the new plate measured 19 x 24in (48.3 x 61cm).
[205] *Whitehall Evening Post*, May. 25-27, 1784; *Morning Herald*, May 26, 1784.

It portrayed part of a recent battle to repell invading French troops from Jersey. Again a figure attired in white is positioned at the centre of a theatrical picture, this figure expiring in the arms of loyal comrades as fighting occurs all around. The similarities to *The Death of Captain Cook* are, perhaps, not coincidental. *The Death of Major Peirson* was commissioned by the entrepreneurial John Boydell, backer for Webber's first edition. Boydell was even planning to have Bartolozzi engrave a print of Copley's picture, for there was money to be made from such work.[206]

1784 also saw the official atlas of Cook's last voyage finally published, and people could not only read what had occurred in the celebrated explorer's travels, but via the detailed illustrations see Pacific peoples going about their daily lives. John Webber's stocks could not be higher around London. He was the artist of the moment.

In late winter 1785, some sixteen months after the second print of *The Death of Captain Cook* was released, newspaper advertisements were spruiking the project's end. Webber and Byrne had ceased production. April then May saw subscribers who had yet to pick up their print being urged to hasten in arranging their collection. Any readers anxious that they had missed the chance to own a copy of this great picture were also assured that a small number of fine impressions were available for purchase at £1/11/6 per print.[207]

Then, in mid-summer, came a startling announcement from the Admiralty. An officially authorised print of Webber's *The Death of Captain Cook* was being published in July 1785.[208] It was

---

[206] The print was engraved by James Heath and published on September 1, 1788, by John and Josiah Boydell of 90 Cheapside. Sales were strong and steady. This saw a second print also engraved, with some etching, by James Heath, historical engraver to the King, and published on April 25, 1796, by John and Josiah Boydell of 90 Cheapside and the Shakspeare Gallery, Pall Mall.

[207] *Morning Chronicle,* Mar. 18, 1784; *Morning Post,* Apr. 17, 1784.

[208] Published under the Act on July 1, 1785, a florid dedication to the Lords of the Admiralty appears in the lower margin.

'engraved by Mssr. Bartolozzi and Byrne,' the notice explained, 'and reduced from their large Print of the same subject to a proper Size, to bind up with the Plates of the Voyage; Printed under the Direction of the Admiralty.'[209] At 12 x 16¼ in (30 x 41 cm), nearly half the plate size of the previous print, this third edition was priced at 7/6 and distributed by no less than Nicols on the Strand, bookseller to the King. As part of the arrangement they had made with with the Admiralty, Webber, Bartolozzi and Byrne were also printing official portraits of Captains Cook and King, priced at 8/- for the pair. At the same time Webber authorised a version of the *Death of Captain Cook* to be released in France for a Continental market, with engravings from another half-size plate produced by the leading print seller François Isabey of Rue de Gèvres au Grand Cour, Paris.[210]

Crossing social, cultural and national barriers, by decade's end *The Death of Captain Cook* was seen by an unrivalled and expanding audience. A budget priced print even appeared around Soho—made on the sly by one of Byrne's assistants who cancelled the second edition's plate by cutting an oval shaped section from the centre which shows only Cook assailed by Hawaiians, and printing just that detail.[211]

A popular topic for conversation, the engraving continued to stimulate talk of Cook's voyages, his scientific discoveries, the strange lands and exotic peoples. Viewers were puzzled by the navigator's gesture in the picture. Is Cook beckoning sailors

---

[209] *Public Advertiser*, July 22, 1785.
[210] Engraved by Claude-Mathieu Fessard, the image measured 8 ⅝ x 11 ¾ in, with the title beneath 'Mort Tragique du CAPITAINE COOK, le 15 Fevrier, 1779, Sur la cote d'Owhy-hee, l'une des Isles Sandwich, decouverte par ce Navigateur.' It included as well a dedication to Bougainville, a brief mention of Cook's achievements, and an explanation of what had prompted the skirmish in Hawaii.
[211] Appearing late in 1785, the engraving was not formally published under the Act, and distributed from a shop (proprietor unknown) at Spur St, on the Soho side of Leicester Square. The reduced plate, which Byrne cut into an oval, measured 14 x 10½in (35 x 26.5cm). Intact copies are rare. The British Museum has a good inpression, while a damaged impression is in the National Library of Australia's Rex Nankivell Collection.

to rescue him, or imploring them to cease shooting? And what should one make of how he stands between soldiers and natives, obstructing musket fire? 'The ambiguity is sufficiently strong,' Bernard Smith explains, 'to support a reading of Cook as a martyr-hero willing to sacrifice his life rather than command the death of his native friends.'[212] Far from being the agent of European expansion, James Cook is shown as wanting to protect Pacific Islanders from it. Tellingly, the Soho print had the words 'a Victim to his own Humanity' appear in the paper margin beneath the image.[213]

With so many copies in circulation, John Webber's depiction of Cook as compassionate peace maker was among the pictorial icons of the age. Where ever one went there were people who had seen it, and were eager to talk: Jefferson and Mozart, Nelson and Goethe, Coleridge and Bonaparte were among those who contemplated Webber's signal image. It had unrivalled reach.

---

[212] Smith, *Imagining the Pacific*, p. 233; Joppien and Smith also write 'His death is portrayed as that of an innocent victim, killed in the act of pleading for peace.' Joppien & Smith, *Art of Captain Cook's Voyages*, vol. 3, p. 126.
[213] Joppien & Smith, op. cit., p. 126.

Index

Account of the Voyages Undertaken ... in the Southern Hemisphere—see John Hawkesworth
Allen, John 4
Admiralty 4, 9, 25-6, 58, 85-86, 94, 96, 96 fn; orders to Cook 25; print of *Death of Captain Cook* 100-101
American colonies 22, 24
Anderson, Dr William 14, 15, 19, 21, 30, 61
animal extinctions 42, 42 fn
Australia 27, 70-71; conflict in 27
Authentic account of the fate of ten men (anon) 55-58

Banks, Joseph 9, 17, 18, 22, 23, 24, 32, 33, 33 fn, 39, 64, 82
Bartolozzi, Francesco RA 94, 98, 100, 101
Bayly, William 12, 18, 51-52, 54, 60, 68,
Bell, Michael 2
Bennett, Robert 95
Between Worlds—see Anne Salmond
Blainey, Geoffrey 65
Bligh, Lt William 5, 21,
Botany Bay 27
Bosch, Cornelis 8, 59
Boswell, James 9
Boydell, John 97, 98, 100
de Bougainville, Louis 36, 42
Bradley, William 46
Brönte, Emily 38

de Brosses, Charles 19
Brown, John 46
Buchan, Alexander 18
Burke, Joseph 87
Burney, Fanny 23, 23 fn
Burney, Lt James 6, 11-12, 23 fn; Search party 1-2, 4, 14-15, 52-54, 55, 58, 59, 64, 65, 68, 74-75; Marra version 49-52, 55-58, 67-68, 69; Dog incident 71-73
Byrne, William 94-95, 96-97, 98, 99, 100, 101

cannibalism 8, 14, 43, 51-54, 57, 64, 67-68; proof 33-34; widows scars 34; *whangui hau* rites 2, 15; human flesh 1, 34, 50, 51, 52, 53, 56, 57, 60, 67, 69
Cape Town 8, 9
Captain Cook's Epic Voyage—see Geoffrey Blainey
Cavenaugh, John 2
Clerke, Cdr Charles 2, 5, 6, 7, 10, 21, 28, 32 fn, 34, 61, 62, 65, 70, 72, 73.
Constable, John 19
Copley, John Singleton 99; *Death of Major Peirson* 99-100
Cook, Cpt James—background and youth 35-38; in London 9, 25, 58; scientific leadership 17-19, 38-39, 90-91; personnel selection 19, 38-39, 88, 90-91; directs artists 16, 19, 82, 83, 88, 91; Naval orders 25-26; ship's discipline 30, 43, 45-46,

59, 63; rules of engagement 26-29, 33; at Queen Charlotte Sound, N.Z. 10-16, 20-22, 83; opposed to vengeance 5-6, 10, 30, 43; meets Kahura 14-16, 43; trade with natives 29-30; relations with natives 3, 5-6, 10-11, 28-29, 31, 40-41, 43, 82-83, 88, 89; distress at future 40; health 31, 64; death 1, 3-4, 7, 10, 96

Cook: From Sailor to Legend—see Robert Mundle

Cook: Master of the Seas—see Frank McLynn

Cotman, John 19

Cox, Matthew 45

Darnton, Robert 73

Death of Captain Cook—see John Webber

Death of Wolfe—see Edward Penny and Benjamin West

Dermot, James 46

Diamond, Jared 42

Diderot, Denis 25

Dodd, D.P. 94

dogs 14, 50, 56, 60, 69, 72, 73, 75, 76, 77

HMS *Dolphin* 61

Douglas, James (Lord Morton) 26-27

Doyle, William 46

Easter Island 5, 41-42, 86

Elliott, Mshp John 59, 62-63

Ellis, John 91

Ellis, William 18

Endeavour River 27, 70-71

environmental degradation 41-42

ethnography 17, 19-20, 21, 81, 90, 93 see also Portraiture

European Enlightenment 22, 26

Facey, William 2

Fannin, Peter 53, 69

FitzSimons, Peter 70-71

Fatchett, Thomas 4

Forster, Dr Georg 18, 27-28, 39, 41, 62, 82-83, 84, 85. 91-82, 93; criticises book illustrations 91-93

Forster, Johann 18, 27, 39, 84, 85

Fressard, Claude-Mathieu 101 fn

Furneaux, Cdr Tobias 1, 4, 5, 8, 12, 51, 68; in London 22

du Fresne, Marc-Joseph Marion 8

Galileo 39

Gauguin, Paul 43

George III 22, 23, 98

Giants 9, 42, 61

Golden Age, see Polynesia—Idealisation of

Gore, Lt John 30

Great Cat Massacre—see Robert Darnton

Green, Charles 32, 32 fn

Gulliver, Lemuel 24

Guns, Germs and Steel—see Jared Diamond

Harvey, Mshp William 6

Hawaii, Kealakekua Bay attack 2-4, 5-7

Hawkesworth, Dr John 9, 19, 42

Hicks, Lt Zachary 30

Hill, Thomas 2, 51, 52, 53
Hinks, Theophilus 4
Histoire des Navigations aux Terres Australes—see Charles des Brosses
historical clairvoyance 71
Historical Epistle from Omaih (anon.) 24-25
Hitihiti 85
Hodges, William 17, 18-19, 87 fn, 91; & landscape art 18 19, 87, esp. 87 fn; & Cook 83; portraits 82-86, 87, 88; Omai portrait 88; *Landing at Middleburgh* 91-92
Hogarth, William 40
Home, Mshp Alexander 61-62, 75-77
Home, Lt George 76
von Humboldt, Alexander 19
Hunter, John 88

Isabey, François 101

James Cook: The Story Behind the Man Who Mapped the World—see Peter FitzSimons
Jeffs, Henry 45
Johnson, Samuel 9 fn, 23
Jones, Edward 2
Joppien, Rüdiger 17, 21 fn, 89
Journal of the Resolution's Voyage—see John Marra

Kahura 2, 12-13, 15, 16, 21, 22, 55, 68, 71; reputation 12, 13, 14; descriptions of 14; meets Cook 43-44; portrait 16-17, 43-44

Kalani'opu'u 3, 7
King, Lt Phillip 5, 6, 10

HMS Lady Penrhyn 90
Lee, Richard 45
Lord Morton, President of Royal Society—see James Douglas
Lord Sandwich, Head of British Navy—see John Montagu

Marra, John 58-60, 61, 68
Matahoua 'Pedro' 21
Maxwell, Mshp James 63
Mayer, Robert 95
McLynn, Frank 49, 54, 55, 59; influence of Salmond 67-68, 71-72
Milton, Thomas 2
Monkhouse, Dr William 32, 70
Montagu, John (Earl of Sandwich) 22-23, 25-26
Mundle, Robert 66, 68
Murphy, Francis 2
musical concerts 66-67

natives killed—Hawaii 7; New Zealand 33; Tonga 30; Vanautu 45
native thefts 2-3, 3 fn, 28, 30, 31
Negro's head—see James Sevilley
New Zealand 10-16, 20-22, 31-34, 40, 74-75, 77-78, 82-84; Grassy Cove attack 1-2, 4-5, 12-13, 51-54
Nicholson, James 45
Noble Savage 8; also see Portraiture; & Polynesia—Idealisation of
North-West Passage 2

Omai 10, 12, 15, 22 fn; abuses Kahura 14, 15-16, 71, 73-74, 78; in London 22-23, 24-25, 25 fn, 86-87, 88; portraits of 22, 23, 86-87, 88
Orientalism—see Edward Said
Orio 85, 93
Otāgo 85, 93

Parkinson, Sydney 17, 18, 81, 90
Patatau 85
Paulaho 89
Penny, Edward RA 95
Pereira [Paroya], Manoel 45
Phillips, Lt Molesworth 3, 4, 96, 98
Pickersgill, Lt Richard 32 fn, 34, 62
Poedua 89
Polynesia—Idealisation of 8, 9, 24-25, 42-43; classicism 9, 36, 87, 92, 94; noble savage 8—see also Portraiture
portraiture 81-86, 88 fn; chalk drawings 82-85; friendship portraits 82, 85, 89-90; diplomatic role 85, 88-89, 90; stylisation issues 86, 87, 91-93; racial types 81-82—see also William Hodges, Joshua Reynolds, John Webber
Price, Mshp Charles 63
Puni 89

Reynolds, Sir Joshua RA 22, 23, 86; Omai portrait 86-87
Riou, Mshp Edward 72, 76, 77, 78
Rousseau, Jean-Jacques 8

Rowe, Mshp James 1, 2, 13, 51, 52, 69; leads shore party 43
Royal Academy 23, 86, 87, 91, 95
Royal Society 22, 25-27, 86, 87; instructions to Cook 26-27

Said, Edward 42-43
Salmond, Anne 49-51, 54, 55, 59-61, 64, 68-70; Dog fixation 50, 60, 69, 72-73
Samwell, David 61, 74, 77-78
Scottish diaspora 36-38
Sevilley, James 2, 51, 52
Sherwin, John Keyes 91, 92
Smith, Bernard 17, 20, 21, 21 fn, 41, 51 fn, 89; Cook as martyr 102
Solander, Dr Daniel 18, 19, 32, 39
Sparrman, Anders 41, 83
Spöring, Herman 18, 81
Stephens, Henry 45
Supplément au Voyage de Bougainville—see Denis Diderot

Tasman, Abel 31-32,
Thomas, James Cpl 4
Thurman [Thurmond], John 45
Tiata 26
Tonga 28, 67; market 29; conflict 28
Tow, William 45
Trevenen, Mshp James 61
Trial of the Cannibal Dog—see Anne Salmond
Tu 85, 89-90
Tupia 32
Tynai-mai 85, 93

Utopianism, see Polynesia—
    Idealisation of

Vancouver, Mshp George 63
venereal disease 30-31, 46, 70

Wales, Williams 8, 18, 41, 84, 92, 93
Webber, John 16, 19-22, 26, 88, 91; political symbolism 21-22, 21 fn, 26, 42, 97-98, 101-102; portraits 89; Kahura portrait 16-17, 43-44, 71, 73, 74, 78, 81, 89; *Captain Cook in Ship Cove* 20-22; *Death of Captain Cook* 20, 80, 94-102; different prints 98-101, 101 fn; publicity 94-95, 96, 100
Wedgeborough, William 45
West, Benjamin RA 95
Whitehouse, John 63
Williamson, Lt John 4, 98
Wilson, Richard 17
Woodhouse, Mshp Thomas 2, 53
Wordsworth, William 65

www.ingramcontent.com/pod-product-compliance
Lightning Source LLC
Chambersburg PA
CBHW050555160426
43199CB00015B/2664